# QUALITY: THE BALL IN YOUR COURT

Also available from ASQC Quality Press

*Benchmarking: The Search for Industry Best Practices That Lead to Superior Performance*
Robert C. Camp

*Management by Policy: How Companies Focus Their Total Quality Efforts to Achieve Competitive Advantage*
Brendan Collins and Ernest Huge

*Policy Deployment: The TQM Approach to Long-Range Planning*
Bruce M. Sheridan

*Breakthrough Quality Improvement for Leaders Who Want Results*
Robert F. Wickman and Robert S. Doyle

*Quality Function Deployment: Linking a Company with Its Customers*
Ronald G. Day

*Where Leadership Begins: Key Skills of Today's Best Managers*
Michael J. Langdon

To request a complimentary catalog of publications, call 800-248-1946.

# QUALITY: THE BALL IN YOUR COURT

Second Edition

Frank C. Collins Jr.

ASQC Quality Press
Milwaukee, Wisconsin

*Quality: The Ball in Your Court*
Second Edition
Frank C. Collins Jr.

Library of Congress Cataloging-in-Publication Data

Collins, Frank C.
    Quality: the ball in your court / Frank C. Collins, Jr. — 2nd
ed.
      p.  cm.
    Includes bibliographical references and index.
    ISBN 0-87389-272-0 (alk. paper)
    1. Quality control—United States.   2. United States—
Manufactures—Quality control.   I. Title.
TS156.C66   1994
659.5'62'0973—dc20                        93-30448
                                                CIP

©1994 by ASQC

10 9 8 7 6 5 4 3 2 1

ISBN 0-87389-272-0

Acquisitions Editor: Susan Westergard
Production Editor: Annette Wall
Marketing Administrator: Mark Olson
Set in Goudy by Montgomery Media, Inc.
Cover design by Montgomery Media, Inc.
Printed and bound by BookCrafters, Inc.

ASQC Mission: To facilitate continuous improvement and increase customer satisfaction by identifying, communicating, and promoting the use of quality principles, concepts, and technologies; and thereby be recognized throughout the world as the leading authority on, and champion for, quality.

For a free copy of the ASQC Quality Press Publications Catalog, including ASQC membership information, call 800-248-1946.

Printed in the United States of America

 Printed on acid-free recycled paper

 ASQC
Quality Press
611 East Wisconsin Avenue
Milwaukee, Wisconsin 53202

*When it is evening, ye say. It will be fair weather: for the sky is red. And in the morning, It will be foul weather today: for the sky is red and lowring. O ye hypocrites, ye can discern the face of the sky; but can ye not discern the signs of the times?*

Matthew 16:2–3 (KJV)

# CONTENTS

# FOREWORD TO THE
# SECOND EDITION

The creation and application of the simple silicon chip has revolutionized the way we live. It has accelerated the advance of technology to a degree difficult to comprehend. No one understands this better than I.

During the Vietnam conflict, as a fighter pilot, I flew into combat with the most advanced fighter at the time—the McDonnell Douglas F-4 Phantom. In combat its twin engines gave us a powerful advantage over the North Vietnamese, who were flying Soviet-designed and manufactured MIGs. While most of our kills were made with missiles, I personally favored the Side-winder heat-seeking store; a somewhat extended version of the World War II dog-fight still prevailed. A couple of decades later, the U.S. military was flying the F-14 Tomcat with Phoenix missiles that could engage an enemy fighter nearly 100 miles away.

Even as technology has changed the nature of aerial combat, the technology of management has likewise changed. Two decades ago, workers by and large were willing to let management make all the decisions. The sign above one executive's desk that read, "Because I'm the boss, that's why," was sufficient reason.

Just as the F-4 has given way to the F-14, 16, and 18, management philosophy of the 1970s has given way to a new management thinking that says, "No one of us is as smart as all of us." Autocratic management is out and participative management is in, and will remain in for the foreseeable future. Empowerment of employees, team problem solving, education and training of all employees, understanding of the importance of the customer, the pre-eminence of individuals, and quality of product or service are the key philosophies that will dominate those companies wishing to be competitive and survive in an extremely competitive international marketplace.

Admiral Frank Collins, a gentleman whom I respect both as a U.S. Navy professional and as a family man who has raised a quality family, has recently updated and expanded this thesis, which I have already alluded to, in his treatise written especially for top management. *Quality: The Ball in Your Court* tells it like it is. Whereas, in the past, management may have been able to "pass the buck" to the union, individual workers, or other bête noires, today if a business fails, management must face up to their own failure. Collins stresses leadership as an essential ingredient for success in business.

From successful fighter pilot and educator, I am now a congressman engaged in perhaps my biggest contest, that of working with my colleagues in the United States 103d Congress, to nurture a competitive spirit in American industry for regaining leadership in manufacturing, which can put people back to work and perpetuate a standard of living that, for future generations, now appears threatened. If you are in management and wish to survive and succeed in the twenty-first century, this book is for you.

Randy "Duke" Cunningham
U.S. House of Representatives

**Author's note:** The Honorable Randy "Duke" Cunningham, a retired U.S. Navy commander, is a second-term congressman who, after a successful career in the field of education, and service to the United States during the Vietnam conflict as a fighter pilot and the first air ace of that war, is still serving the country he loves in the 103d Congress as the representative for the 51st Congressional District of California. He is a member of the House Armed Services Committee, House Committee on Education and Labor, and the House Merchant Marine and Fisheries Committee.

# FOREWORD TO THE FIRST EDITION

I have been reading essays of quality production for several years, and written a few myself. This book, by Frank Collins, is the best I have seen. But it rests on a mystery.

No American businessman opposes this theme; none is opposed to turning out goods and services of high quality. Indeed, many believe they are doing so and have been doing so for quite some time.

Yet, with a few exceptions, most are simply *not* doing it. The telltale sign is our deficit in world trade, our national failure to compete in quality and price with the output of other nations. That deficit increases year by year. As I write, it has reached about $170 billion for the year, the biggest shortfall in trade ever registered by any nation in history.

It has meant that more and more of our industries are cutting wages, laying off workers, curtailing production, moving abroad—or simply giving up and closing shop altogether.

At first the decline affected basic industries, steel, autos, machine tools. Then the disappearance of American producers from consumer electronics, like TV sets and microwave ovens, became conspicuous. Now the high-tech basics—semiconductors, those little memory chips, are going fast. It is ironic that, as I write, Fairchild, one of the two companies that invented the miraculous little chips, is under bid for purchase by a Japanese company.

It is sad to contemplate that if there were a world emergency, and we were called on to become the arsenal of democracy again, we probably could not do it.

The excuses generally given for our failure to compete have, one by one, been discredited:

The value of the dollar rose too high in relation to other currencies, making our exports too expensive to sell, and imports from other nations so cheap that they flooded our markets and put our businesses, making the same things, out of business.

Well, at this writing the dollar has fallen radically for two years, and the deficits have gone on growing. Clearly the expensive dollar was an excuse, not a cause.

Low wages gave the Japanese an advantage our high-wage businesses could not compete with.

I have on my desk a copy of *The Economist*, whose cover displays a large Japanese holding a small Uncle Sam in his palm, saying, "We are richer than you." The article inside states that unit labor costs in Japan now exceed those in the United States, and the average Japanese income has reached $17,000 to American's $16,000.

The Japanese beat us by resorting to unfair trade practices.

Well, the U.S. government has given special protections to industries that have made that assertion. Yet foreign cars take away more of the U.S. market every passing year. As this is written, General Motors—after pouring over $30 billion into automation and reorganization—has announced plans to close so many plants that another 10 percent of our market may be ceded to foreigners.

No, the truth has to be that our oral dedication to quality production is again, with a few exceptions, not being realized by action.

Why have we been failing in a field of endeavor in which we once excelled? I suggest that the principal reason is a psychological cycle that has become almost commonplace in American history. We have been an unusually successful nation. But our success has bred complacency and self-satisfaction.

Our last huge success was in not just winning World War II, but emerging from it with the only unbombed, undamaged, booming national economy left in the world. A wrecked world came to us to beg, borrow, or buy the means of survival. Such was the demand for American goods and services for about 30 years that our leaders—whether in politics or business—began to assume that U.S. economic superiority was part of the natural order of things.

There are a thousand illustrative examples. Typical of all was the visit in 1954 by Secretary of State John Foster Dulles to Premier Yoshida in Tokyo. Mr. Dulles told the Japanese prime minister—it was reported in every newspaper at the time—that Japan had best abandon the hope of finding markets in the United States. Japan simply did not know how to make things Americans wanted to buy. Japan, he said, must seek markets in the underdeveloped world. Well, we know what happened to that prophecy and that advice.

The hour is late for America to recover from our illusions and learn to compete. If you wish to understand the problem, and learn what to do, read on.

Howard K. Smith
Bethesda, Maryland
January 1987

# PREFACE

*Quality* is one of the most common clichés used in advertising nowadays. Whether you are buying hamburgers or mudguards, the buzzword is *quality*. It is also one of today's most written-about subjects, as a look through the newsstands or bookshelves will reveal. And quality is now the subject of more conferences, seminars, and special retreats than at any previous time.

Regrettably, advertising quality, writing about the subject, or meeting to talk about the idea alone will not restore quality to American products and services. Should we conclude, then, that there is no way from here to there? Emphatically not!

There is a way to restore America to its traditional economic vitality: by returning to the quality course that leads to job satisfaction, market competition, and economic advantage. To achieve this status, we must teach the right people—those who control the resources—to understand their responsibilities and provide them with the *keys to quality*: It is for the men and women who are responsible for the make-or-break decisions in industry and business—both manufacturing and service—that this book has been written and updated.

Frank C. Collins Jr.
Rear Admiral, U.S. Navy (Ret)
Alexandria, Virginia
September 1992

# ACKNOWLEDGMENTS

Completion of this book has been a shared achievement, for which I am indebted to many people. At the outset, I would like to recognize just a few of those who have made this book possible.

First, I would like to recognize the Bureau of Naval Personnel, who posted me as its executive director, quality assurance, to the Defense Logistics Agency (DLA) as my last flag assignment. What I accepted as a poor second choice to a cruiser destroyer flotilla command turned out to be one of the most absorbing, exciting, and challenging in a 33-year span of such assignments.

This book is also dedicated to . . .

- All of my colleagues at DLA—and especially Col. Lloyd Gimple, USA (Ret), Ernie Ellis, Bernie Mahar, and the other quality professionals in DLA-Q; Vice Admiral Eugene Grinstead, SC USN (Ret), my boss; and Don Moore, my deputy; Frank Carlucci and Paul Thayer, both former deputy secretaries of defense who supported our Bottom-Line Conferences (BLCs); Drs. Joseph Juran, A. V. "Val" Feigenbaum, Al Gunneson, and Stu Hunter, all of whom participated so effectively in those defense/industry quality dialogues; and to the scholarly dean of U.S. news reporters, Howard K. Smith, for the superb job he did of translating a day's BLC dialogue into a pithy anchorman's wash-up;
- Bob Bauman, chairman of Beecham Group P.L.C. and former chairman and CEO of Avco Corp., who determined that his legacy to Avco would be a quality culture and brought me aboard to help him implement it; Don Farrar, senior executive vice president of Textron and past president of Avco, for his unflagging support and participation in the Avco

quality improvement process; and to Avco's 11 major division presidents who cooperated in implementing individual quality improvement processes at their units;

- Ed Graham, who was my associate at Textron and executive assistant during my tour as chief naval advisor to CINC Imperial Iranian Navy and as executive director of DLA, for his wise and thoughtful counsel;
- My guides in Japan, Junko "Julie" Miyata and "Mike" Matsueda, and my interpreters, Noriko Hosoyamada and Kumiko Kato;
- My many Japanese, Korean, European, and Canadian friends and counselors in industry, including the late Dr. Kaoru Ishikawa, president of Musashi Institute of Technology; Dr. S. Inaba, president of Fanuc; Osamu Takahashi, executive managing director of Komatsu; "Terry," Tony, and Tom Yamazaki, Yamazaki Mazak Corp.—president, executive vice president, and senior vice president, respectively; Yuzo Kojima, general manager of Toshiba's Fuchu plant; Junji Noguchi, executive director of the Union of Japanese Scientists and Engineers (JUSE); K. Goshi, chairman emeritus, and Mioki Aoki, secretary general, Japan Productivity Center; Takeo Yamoka, president of Tokyo Juki Industrial Co.; Dr. Ryuji Fukuda, adviser to Japan Management Association and author of *Managerial Engineering*; and Dr. Avigdor Zonnenshain, director, Quality Assurance, RAFAEL in Haifa, Israel—all of whom provided me with insights into quality offshore;
- My 16,000+ DOD contractors, many of whom I was able to visit and exchange ideas with during my years at DLA;
- My ASQC reviewers and Kelley Cardinal and Annette Wall at ASQC for their observations and suggestions;
- Peggy Thompson, whose editorial advice I value highly;
- And, finally, to my dear wife, Esther, who supported me so faithfully on this project by being my chief adviser and typing most of the raw manuscript. Her biggest sacrifice was giving me up to the chore of writing and revising this book on *her* time. To me, it was a labor of love and concern for this country; to Esther, a sacrifice of our scarce time together.

To all of you mentioned by name, and to the hundreds of unnamed friends and associates who have influenced me and given me input for this book, my sincere and heartfelt thanks.

# INTRODUCTION

Japan has fascinated me since my first visit as a young Navy lieutenant operations officer on the *Henry W. Tucker* DDR 875 in November 1956. I have been an avid Japan watcher in the many subsequent visits I have made to that unique and beautiful island nation. I love the Japanese as a people and am intrigued by their industry and by their culture with its attention to detail. There is still much we can learn from them.

During my 1982 and 1983 visits, my status as the executive director of quality assurance for the Defense Logistics Agency encouraged a great freedom of exchange, since I was an official visitor and not a competitor. I visited more than 30 industries and institutions and talked to countless individuals.

The following is a partial listing: the late Dr. Kaoru Ishikawa, president, Musashi Institute of Technology (MIT), Tokyo and Dr. M. Imaizumi, also of MIT; Junji Noguchi, Union of Japanese Scientists and Engineers (JUSE); Kohei Goshi and Mikio Aoki, Japan Productivity Center; Fujitsu Corp. (Kawasaki plant); Yokogawa Hewlett-Packard (Hachiooji); Nissan Motors (Oppama and Murayama auto plants); Nissan Aeronautical and Space Division; Nippon Kokan K.K. (Keihin steel works); Komatsu (Tokyo, Kawasaki, Awazu, and Komatsu plants); Ministry of International Trade and Industry (MITI); Nikon (F3 and F3AF assembly plants); Toshiba (Fuchu plant); Fanuc (Fuji); Nippon Electric Co. (NEC), Fuchu plant; Ishikawajima-Harima Heavy Industries (IHI), Mizuko plant (aerospace and engines); IHI Tokyo Shipyard Division; Sanyo Shokai (Tokyo); Kawasaki Heavy Industries (Gifu and Akashi); Yamazaki Mazak Corp. (Oguchi-cho); Mazak Century 21 Automated Factory of the Future (Minokomo); (Ichinomiya); Kyocera Ceramics (Shiga Gamoo); Kulicke and Soffa Ltd. (Tokyo); Sumitomo

(Tokyo); Fuji Bank (Tokyo); Nitsuko (Shiroishi); Tokyo Juki Industrial Co. (Ohtawara and Chofu City plants); Nomura Research Institute; and Yasuda Fire and Marine Insurance Co. (Tokyo).

During my visit in 1982, I first noted Japanese amusement about U.S. industry's curiosity about Japan's *quality secret.* The Japanese candidly shared their secret, generously crediting contributions by Deming, Juran, and Feigenbaum. Needless to say, not all of Japan's success can be traced to its ability to follow directions. In fact, during visits in 1982–1983, I, along with my executive assistant, Commander Ed Graham, and our American Japanese translator, Peggy Otsuka, determined that at least 40 factors accounted for Japanese success in quality. After visits in 1984–1985, I revised that figure upward to 60.

During 1982–1984, I visited Europe on three occasions to examine quality on the continent. My visits were limited to Citroen, Avions Marcel Dassault Brequet Aviation (three plants); Souriau and CIE; MAN; Zettelmeyer; MATRA; Aerospatial; Teleforban and Normalzeit; Battelle Institute; and Surveillance Industrielle de l'Armement (SIAR).

In 1983, I observed Korean industries and learned much about this awakening giant as I visited, among others, Oriental Precision Co.; Hyosung Heavy Industries Ltd.; Gold Star Precision Co.; KIA Industrial Co. Ltd.; Korean Standards Association—all of the foregoing in Seoul—and Korean Airlines (Pusan); Daewoo Shipbuilding and Heavy Machinery Ltd. (Okpo); Gold Star Precision Co. (Gumi); Samsung Electronics (Kyunghi); Pohang Iron and Steel Co. (Pohang); and Kukje Corp. (Pusan).

I had the privilege of visiting five of China's major industrial cities during a three-week tour in 1985. Beginning in Beijing and moving to Tianjin, Dalian, Shenyang, and finally to Quanzhou, we visited and spoke to many audiences and in many factories. Among them were Beijing Renmin Machinery Plant, #2 Chemical Works, Second Pharmaceutical Factory, Battery Factory, Shirt Factory, and Machine Works; Tianjin Radio Factory, Carpet Factory #3, and Orthopedic Instrument Factory; Dalian Shipyard and Dalian Machinery Plant; Shenyang Heavy Machinery Plant and Heavy Machinery Plant Foundry; Quanzhou Electric Institute; and Far East Electric Fan Factory. We also spoke to large audiences at the International Club in Beijing, Tianjin Quality Control Association, Tianjin University, Quanzhou Labor Union Meeting Hall, and Jinan University.

I have made subsequent trips to speak in Korea, Japan, Hong Kong, and Israel during the period 1985–1992, where I have learned a great deal more which has been folded into this compendium of advice to top management. My teaching visits to Israel's RAFAEL company were especially meaningful.

This book was written to examine quality abroad and at home and to suggest courses of action to improve quality in the United States. After spending 33 years in the U.S. Navy, the author recognizes that readers may find his language a bit salty. I hope that this does not detract from the contents. To help the uninitiated over some of the acronyms, I have added a glossary as Appendix F. In addition, when the book was originally published, the Department of Defense (DOD) was the United States' largest business, and many of the references used are about defense, or defense-related, issues. However, I believe the references are still valid since, despite assertions to the contrary, communism in the world is far from dead, and the Confederation of Independent States (CIS) is by no means a stable institution. While DOD spending may be shrinking, the issue of quality still relates to our economic survival, defense readiness, and success as a free nation and world leader in the twenty-first century. The courses of action recommended here will be presented in language that every echelon of management can understand. They provide, in general and specific terms, the how to of changing the course of economic history. The time for action is now.

# 1 QUALITY: AMERICA'S DILEMMA

## THE WORLD'S OLDEST PROFESSION

Many mistakenly believe that prostitution is the world's oldest profession. Others, harking back to the garden scene, claim marketing (the serpent was having a sale on apples). Interestingly enough, neither prostitution nor sales (I guess both are in the marketing category) can claim to be first. Actually, the world's oldest documented profession is quality.

Genesis 1:31 gives us a widely accepted reference: ". . . and God looked at all that He had made, and it was very good. . . ."[1] *The essence of quality is described.* The conceptualizer, designer, builder, and marketer of the universe did a first-article inspection and declared that it had turned out just as He had planned.

Another early reference on quality is the Code of Hammurabi, attributed to the Babylonian king whose reign—accepted as being 1728–1686 B.C.—marked the beginning of the first golden age of Babylon. His code, inscribed in an eight-foot-high pillar of black diorite, was discovered at Susa in 1902; it has numerous examples of the high esteem accorded quality workmanship.

> "If a boatman caulked a boat for a seigneur and did not do the boat well with the result that the boat has sprung a leak in the very year, since it has developed a defect, the boatman (builder) shall dismantle that boat and strengthen it at his own expense . . . ."
>
> (Article 234)[2]

1

Was this the first recorded warranty? Or consider this persuasive motivation to do it right the first time:

> "If a builder constructed a house but did not make his work strong with the result that the house which he built collapsed and so caused the death of the owner of the house, the builder shall be put to death."
>
> (Article 229)[3]

The Chinese appear to have institutionalized quality from the standpoint of government inspection as far back as the Ch'in dynasty: ". . . the penalty for poor quality ranged from a public lashing to fines and detonation of goods."[4]

## TODAY'S PRIORITY

Quality is a priority concern in this country today. Perhaps more now than at any time in the past, the lack of quality in goods and services is having a serious impact economically in view of the market share and jobs we have already lost to foreign competitors through inattention to quality. The automotive, electronics, steel, shipbuilding, and appliances industries have seen the heaviest losses, with optics, clothing, textiles, and footwear coming in for substantial shares. Regrettably, it appears that the answer to foreign competition is for U.S. companies to have cars, engines, sewing machines, or TVs made by a foreign producer and marketed with a U.S. trade name. While this may make the product more competitive with foreign-label goods, it brings back not a single production job to our country.

Another ploy our competitors have used effectively to make their competition more palatable has been to build their plants in the United States and use U.S. workers. Sony, Nissan, Toyota, and Honda are examples of this approach. Interestingly, very few key *executives* at these plants are Japanese, but their stated goal is to turn out a better product than their parent organizations in Japan. My observation has been that American workers, under Japanese management techniques, equal or exceed their competition, the Japanese worker.

These efforts affect our balance of payments. After years of being a nation of exporters—supplying not only raw materials but finished goods—we have become a nation that, according to Department of Commerce statistics as of first quarter 1993, had a $10.49 billion trade deficit, considerably improved over the $83.9 billion trade deficit in the first half of 1986.[5]

**Impact on Military Readiness**

From a standpoint of military readiness, quality is exacting an unacceptable toll. Paul Thayer, former deputy secretary of defense, has called scrap rates of 10–30 percent a *surcharge*—an added cost that makes it more difficult for the DOD to economize, particularly in the face of justified additional requirements. In addition, consider the effect on the morale of our troops when they see the poor performance of the M60 A-2 tank compared to the Soviet T-64. That morale problem is difficult to price out. General P. X. Kelly, former commandant, USMC, very succinctly summarized the issue of quality when he stated, "The failure of a weapon in combat doesn't just mean that you return it to the factory for repair. It normally means that someone will be killed . . . . I merely ask that you take a close look at the quality of your product . . . and recognize that its success or failure can well mean life or death on the battlefield."[6] Frank Carlucci, then deputy secretary of defense, made the same point: "There can be no product recalls on the battlefield. No time for warranty work. The lives of American servicemen and women are on the line."[7]

It is hardly right for us to ask our military to keep the peace—with all the rigors, risks, and deprivations that charge represents—while we are unwilling to provide them with quality weapons and support systems.


## INDUSTRY STATUS

To get an idea of the current status of quality, let's look at two key industry segments that have had widely publicized quality problems: automakers and defense contractors.

**The Auto Industry**

The U.S. automobile is perhaps the most easily recognized victim of the quality campaign waged by the Japanese. The proliferation of Toyota, Nissan, Subaru, and Isuzu cars and trucks on U.S. highways is ample evidence of the success of their campaigns. A former Ford automotive executive candidly explained to me that, "We ignored the potential economic impact of the gas crunch of the early 70s. We didn't foresee that it would dissuade American car buyers from continuing their love affair with the luxurious gas hog, so we didn't develop more fuel-efficient models. We continued to produce and push the big car. We did it to ourselves," he sadly concluded.

The Japanese, standing in the wings with a compact car that was not only fuel efficient but also engineered and manufactured with a discriminating customer in mind, wooed the American buyer who was fed up with the built-in obsolescence of U.S. autos. This is likely to be a long and happy marriage. Quotas and tariffs will neither dissuade Americans from buying cars that represent quality of workmanship and reliability, nor persuade them to buy U.S. automobiles marketed on the basis of $2000 to $2500 rebates and option gimmickry.

The auto industry has exacerbated the situation and lent credence to the myth that we cannot compete quality-wise with the Japanese culture by having components, and even total systems, built in Japan. But putting Big Three labels on what are essentially Japanese-built cars does nothing to regain jobs. The auto industry's current problem is management's indifference, not only to the customer and his or her desires, but also to what is going on down on the factory floor. Increasing return on investment and stockholder romancing have transcended the single most important responsibility of management: determining what the customer wants and satisfying that craving.

A major U.S. auto giant recently spent significant sums of money hiring the most prestigious prophets of quality to set it on a course to regain the American customer's favor. When asked what their priorities were, managers properly indicated quality as number one, ROI for stockholders as number two, and job satisfaction for workers as number three. It was suggested that swapping priorities number two and number three might be a more reasonable approach; with job satisfaction moved up to number two, stockholders' interests would be predictably achieved.

While acknowledging the logic of such a suggestion, management was cautious about bumping the stockholders to number three in the list of company priorities. The stockholders' function of providing capital is essential; nevertheless, the product that provides ROI is made by the workers—from designers at technical centers to mechanics at brand-name dealerships. For too long now, the worker has been considered important—but not the most important cog in manufacturing. The term *worker* includes not only the production worker, but also the designer, production and quality engineers, marketing and sales force, repair technicians, and customer service personnel.

### Defense Industry Impressions
Between 1981 and 1983, as executive director, quality assurance, Defense Logistics Agency, I had the opportunity to visit over 240 industries, with

products ranging from clothing and textiles to the space shuttle, in plants located in the United States, Canada, Japan, Korea, Germany, and France. I was allowed to visit production lines, query people running the machines, talk to quality personnel, and, most importantly, speak to top management. Two hundred five of my visits were to defense industries within the continental United States.

My criteria in assessing the attitude and capacity for quality production contained some 15 to 20 factors. But, I honed in on six that are key to functional achievement of productivity-enhancing quality. They are:

1. Percent of plants with top management who appeared to understand the essence of quality
2. Percent of plants with effective systems for documenting scrap and rework costs
3. Percent of plants with effective formal training programs
4. Percent of plants with functioning quality circles
5. Percent of plants with aggressive automation and/or robotization systems or plans
6. Percent of plants with effective systems for evaluating the effectiveness of a quality program

My initial analysis—done after visiting some 175 plants from the latter part of 1981 through mid-1982—indicated that in some 53 percent of the plants, management appeared to understand who was responsible for quality and how it was achieved. By contrast, some 88 percent of managers spoke convincingly about quality in the last 86 plants visited from mid-1982 through mid-1983. This would appear to point to an upturn in defense quality, since quality depends on top management's perception of its importance and willingness to supply policy and resources needed to achieve quality.

As a private consultant and speaker, I continue to visit and talk with top managers. They have certainly learned to speak the language of quality in this final decade of the twentieth century, and they have become quite interested in total quality management (TQM) since the DOD decreed that it would be the sine qua non of winning DOD contracts. Unfortunately, I continue to find few top managers willing to pay the up-front costs of involvement and money or to invest the time needed for the gestation of the TQM concept.

## QUALITY AFFECTS AND EFFECTS

### Scrap and Rework

The picture was much less cheery in the *hidden factory* area. In the initial survey, only 15 percent had plans for documenting scrap and rework. Most recognized the need for and were in the process of installing some kind of collection system. However, there also was a significant number who felt scrap and rework (S&R) was such a small item as to preclude the need to set up a collection system.

This reasoning misses the primary reason for documenting S&R—to correct problems. While the data will show the magnitude of problems (and, incidentally, should be compared to the cost of manufacturing rather than percentage of sales—to emphasize the point more graphically to management, and, we hope, enlist aid to supporting quality with resources), the data can do far more by identifying *where* S&R is occurring. Follow-up can determine whether a deficiency is caused by lack of training, inadequate equipment, poor design, improper process control, failure to acquire best materials, or poor supplier support. By use of Pareto analysis—an analytical approach to looking at data that Juran has dubbed the "vital few versus the trivial many"—management can decide what to attack and how much effort to assign. Without data, one has no accurate way of determining what needs to be done.

The hidden factory consists of much more than scrap and rework. Appendix B boils down the essential few and gives one formula for determining how effective the quality system you pay for really is. Unfortunately, not a single plant of the 243 had a totally satisfactory means of evaluating its quality system. The difficulty is obvious: the hidden factory adds costs in a great variety of areas. But trying to eliminate all of those costs would be self-defeating.

### Training

There are as many perceptions of the need for and value of formal training as there are people being queried on this point. Few would agree that training is unnecessary in today's world of numerically controlled (NC) and computer numerically controlled (CNC) industrial machinery. Unfortunately, there are too many opinions on how to do it and how much is enough when training is the subject.

To be effective, training must be formalized, structured, and audited at regular intervals. The Edel-Brown Company, in Everett, Massachusetts, serves as an example. This modest-sized machine shop has classrooms and a structured apprentice curriculum that ensures standards in training. Raymond Engineering, in Middletown, Connecticut, a producer of scientific and military recording devices, has an audit system that precludes workers failing to maintain certification or getting into production jobs without proper qualifications. Many companies, however, consider on-the-job training adequate, but more often than not, the quality of such training is insufficient. Of the 157 plants initially visited, only 25 percent had any type of formal training program. Sixty-seven percent of the remaining 86 companies had implemented effective training plans.

The decline in the excellence of our education system over the past two decades has obviously affected quality. Inability to read or perform simple math computations sorely hinders understanding of manufacturing procedures.

### Quality Circles
Perhaps the question that drew the most blank looks was the one on quality circles. "Oh, you mean that Japanese gimmick?" was the other major reaction. Only 16.4 percent of the first group visited indicated that they had quality circles; regrettably, in most cases, few of those companies had any idea of what to expect or how to implement them effectively. Unfortunately, many circles died aborning. Obviously, the word about their value must have spread because 51 percent of the plants visited in the second group claimed to be using quality circles to enhance quality.

### Robots and Automation
While the United States has led the field in development of automation and robots, we have fallen behind in updating our industrial base with them. Only 17.6 percent of the first group had an aggressive automation/robotization plan. The excuses given: "We are waiting for the economy to improve," and "We need help from the government before we can improve our capability in that area."

It is not only simplistic, but futile, to believe the economy will improve before we become more competitive quality-wise. Automation and robotics provide the ability to replicate a product at a competitive production rate. Both systems reduce the possibility of human error.

During my second group of visits, aggressive improvement in the areas of robotics and automation were found in 24 percent of the plants, a figure still much too low.

**The Customer As a Quality Problem**
Willis J. "Will" Willoughby, quality and reliability "czar" for the Navy's now-defunct Material Command, sums up the customer's contribution to poor quality with one phrase: "We get what we accept." Without customer feedback, many producers blithely conclude that there is no problem. In other words, while the house burns, they fiddle because the smoke alarm hasn't alerted them to their situations.

Warranties give everything a false sense of security; they negatively affect both makers and users. Implying value and the manufacturer's concern for the user, the warranty influences customers when they are deciding which product to buy. However, a combination of our national affluence—which makes replacement easier than the hassle of return—and lack of responsiveness of the warrantor renders most warranties totally ineffective as far as feedback to the producer is concerned.

How many times have you read the fine print on the guarantee or warranty, only to discover that it is cheaper to buy a new item than to pack up the old one and pay postage plus the handling charge? Let me give you a personal example. I recently purchased a new color TV manufactured by one of U.S. industry's most-hallowed names. Within six months, a printed circuit board went bad. There would be no charge for the board, I discovered, but the installation would be $50—even though, in my opinion, the manufacturer had a moral responsibility to repair the set without charge. It took me two letters and three phone calls before the maker finally agreed to reimburse me for the charge on the TV set. A less-tenacious customer would have given up sooner. This game is also played by industry outside the United States.

Customers' indifference to poor quality cannot be overlooked. If customers do not pursue their rights under a warranty, they will get what they deserve.

The issue of warranties has two sides: Often, the customer abuses the terms of a warranty, causing the warrantor to become defensive. But would it not be more profitable in the long run to risk an occasional rip-off by a dishonest customer than to fracture the loyalty of an honest one by making it difficult, if not impossible, to get satisfaction? Consider Sears' policy of "customer satisfaction guaranteed." They have made it pay off by selling back defective merchandise to vendors—a valid and logical procedure.

When the government is the customer, it is in a unique position to influence quality. Unfortunately, that influence is often bad. The federal government sometimes buys items that are beyond the state of the art in production technology. To compound the problem, we decide that we cannot live another five years without this answer to all of our operational problems; as a result, we decree minimum development and production time. As must be readily apparent, when the time crunch is on, the first thing to suffer is quality. As a result, we live with an immature design or an inadequately supported system, and blame failures on the manufacturer.

During one visit to the West Coast, I asked a general manager of a large company how he reacted to a "too-short" contract requirement. "We bring it to the procurement contract officer's attention." "And how does he react?" I asked. "He tells us, 'In that case, we would be unresponsive and may feel free not to bid.'" "And do you?" I asked naively. "Of course not. We bid. We have to survive," he answered without hesitation.

## Quality's Impact on the Economy

Poor quality undermines productivity and contributes to inflationary pressures. Wage increases can only fuel inflation when they are not tied to increased productivity. As has been evident in the automobile industry, poor quality wipes out jobs as foreign competition causes buyers to seek a product made abroad. Few people who look objectively at the situation Detroit created for itself a decade ago will dispute the fact that many of the jobs lost to Japanese and European auto industries will never return to the United States. This is sad, particularly because it could have been prevented.

Poor quality further undermines our national reputation as a producer of top-notch goods. Most of us can remember the poor reputation Japanese products had. "Made in Japan" was the *sine qua non* of cheap and oftentimes shoddy goods. Now we can find a Japanese electronics firm rejecting up to 30 percent of the components shipped by its American parent—which, incidentally, may have a very good reputation for high quality. Why the high rejection rate? Because the U.S. parent did not meet Japanese standards.

Reputation is an intangible difficult to set a value on. Loss of reputation results, however, in a loss of market share and buyer confidence. Consider that only three decades ago the United States was a world leader in quality in automobiles and electronics, with Germany holding that title in optics and Switzerland in watches. Now, in all four, Japan is the acknowledged leader.

## WHO'S AT FAULT?

Assessing fault is not nearly as simple as it might seem at first blush. It appears that we all have a piece of the action. Industry, as the producer, must accept a lion's share of the blame for poor quality. But, unions, the consumer, government, marketers, lawyers, and design and production engineers all play significant roles in the issue. Quality is a team effort that involves all hands. If we are to lick the poor quality issue in the United States during this decade, we must candidly evaluate the factors that contribute to poor quality and attack each one. We must not harken to the piper who says there is only one factor and one remedy to correct the situation. If the problem is not solved in this decade, it may well be too late.

Perhaps the most difficult problem relating to quality today is a lack of understanding that quality is not just an acceptable product that comes off the end of an assembly line or service from an office. Rather, quality must be a way of life, because achievement is the joint effort of the producer and customer alike.

## NOTES

1.  *Holy Bible*, King James Version (New York: Thomas Nelson, 1970), 1.

2.  James B. Pritchard, ed., *Ancient Near-Eastern Texts Relating to the Old Testament* (Princeton: Princeton University Press, 1950), 163–180.

3.  Ibid.

4.  Ren Djou, "Historical Episodes About China's Quality Control of Weapons in Chou-Li-Kon Ge," *World Quality Congress Proceedings*, 1984, 179.

5.  Robert Laird, "Our Growing Trade Deficit," *USA Today*, July 30, 1986, sec. 1, p. 1.

6.  Speech by General P. X. Kelly (USMC) at Bottom-Line Conference sponsored by Defense Logistics Agency, Washington, D.C., at Fort McNair, May 13, 1982.

7. Speech by Frank Carlucci at Bottom-Line Conference sponsored by Defense Logistics Agency, Washington, D.C., at Fort McNair, May 13, 1982.

# 2 QUALITY EXAMINED

## QUALITY DEFINED

Trying to define *quality* can be as frustrating as trying to tack gelatin to the wall. Robert Prisig, in his provocative book, *Zen and the Art of Motorcycle Maintenance*, spends some 373 pages trying to define, describe, and explain how quality is achieved.[1] In the *American Heritage Dictionary*, the number of lines defining *quality* is equalled by the number of lines giving synonyms.[2] "The essential character of something; nature" is its preferred definition, while "degree or grade of excellence" rates slot three.

Quality professionals use a variety of definitions. "Meeting the customer's expectations," "compliance with customer's specifications," and "fitness for use" are three popular and generally accepted ones. (See Appendix C for other definitions.) W. Edwards Deming, considered by many to be America's foremost authority on quality, offers this definition: "Good quality means a predictable degree of uniformity and dependability at low cost, with quality suited to the market." Major Gen. A. G. Rogers, USAF, former deputy chief of staff/logistics for the Tactical Air Command, has suggested that "quality translates technology into combat capability."[3] The early 1991 successes in Operation Desert Storm certainly support this premise. I believe that Gen. Rogers' quote could be altered to read, "Quality translates technology into industry strength and market superiority."

My own definition is, "Quality is profit to the maker, value to the user, and satisfaction to both." This means that quality creates a win-win situation; it erases the we-they adversarial relationship that too often infiltrates the quality equation. In the final analysis, customers define quality. They do this in two ways: by continuing their business relationships with you if they are satisfied with your understanding of their quality requirements, and by taking their business elsewhere, refusing to pay, or threatening suit if you don't make good. The latter responses are fairly accurate indicators that your perception of quality does not coincide with your customers' perceptions.

Perhaps a good starting point is to take a moment to decide how you would define quality—as a top manager, as a line supervisor, as an assembler, and then as a customer. Are there marked differences among the four perceptions? Probably so, and this, I believe, is the crux of the quality problem in America and elsewhere today.

Top management, preoccupied with stockholders' interests, sees return on investment multiplying as production costs and time are reduced. Not replacing that tempering oven or not introducing NC or CNC or that new flexible machining center the Yamazaki MAZAK Co. (MAZAK) salesperson has been describing—all are means of cutting capital investment. The result is a stronger short-term bottom line, even if more and more of the product has to be brought to a material review board. As long as the company can ship, that's what matters. Poor quality is shrewd business.

On the line, the line supervisor muses, "What exactly does management want of us? There's no published quality policy, and the production boss sounds like a Marine drill instructor with that constant 'Move it, move it, move it.' I guess as long as I can get it by the review board, I'm satisfying requirements."

The electronics board assembler may reason, "Well, they haven't fired me, so I guess I'm doing okay."

The customer, of course, has other ideas: "Here comes my shipment from the Bare Minimum Company, late as usual and marginal, I'm sure. I've half a mind to return this shipment, pointing out how far off spec the product is. But, since their shipment is late and I need those components to complete my production schedule, I guess I'm stuck with them again. However, I think I'll give Quality First, Inc., a call and see if they would be interested in supplying me. I've heard they concentrate on quality and schedule and are also competitive in price."

Far-fetched musings? Not really. Perhaps the proliferation of definitions has created the communications gap between design and production, between production and quality, between quality and top management, between company and customer.

Advertisers do little to clarify the situation. On the contrary, they appear to add confusion in their overuse of the word *quality* to sell products that can claim innovation only on the basis of styling intended to satisfy the jaded curiosity of a younger generation that has been surfeited by too much, too soon.

Trying to sell a poor product on the basis of quality merely causes greater confusion and cynicism on the part of the buying public. Leaf through a popular magazine and note how many ads use the word *quality* to sell the product. Tonight, while you are watching TV, count the number of times *quality* is used and evaluate its appropriateness in describing the product. These overuses cause the whole meaning of quality to fade into a meaningless blur.

### *Quality* Is a Complex Term

From a user's standpoint, the concept of quality boils down to simple satisfaction with the appearance, performance, and reliability of the product—taking into account the price range that consumer can afford. This doesn't mean having to buy a Rolls Royce or Mercedes to enjoy a quality car. Chevys, Fords, and Plymouths should also represent quality, that is, satisfactory appearance, satisfactory performance, and advertised reliability. Our auto industry for too long has focused on appearance and appointments and neglected engineering and production for performance and reliability. If you have ever tried to change spark plugs or an oil filter in any late model car, you know what I mean.

The first step in achieving quality is defining it as the customers do—understanding and meeting the customers' needs and desires. If a gulf exists between what they think they have ordered and what you deliver, this is scored as a sure quality strikeout. More time in market research or in studying the request for proposal or invitation to bid, and a thorough engineering analysis of the specifications both by design and production to determine your capability to produce, may be worth millions in legal suits or lost sales or follow-on contracts. The key here is communication and documentation. Know what your customers want and ensure that they know what you are going to deliver.

Doing so is particularly important when you are bidding on a conceptual development contract. Often an eager marketer, anxious to sell a company's superiority, will suggest improvements neither stipulated in the concept proposal or within the firm's engineering capability to produce. Similarly, engineers—eager to push the state of the art—will improve the concept to the detriment of the desired system. The key, again, is to know what the customers want—and give it to them.

Herein lies the edge Japanese and European manufacturers have gained.

Yuzo Kojima, general manager of Toshiba Corporation's Fuchii plant, explained the involved process of communication between the customer and Toshiba's design, manufacturing, and quality engineers *before* a new product is committed to production. He said that this is the critical first step toward satisfying the customer.

The second step is equally critical: the transition from design to production. This may be one of America's most serious pitfalls on the road to profitable production.

**Design-Production Transition**

The design-production transition plagues industry. While advanced technology affords design engineers great confidence in their ability to *create* almost anything they want, *producing* it is quite another thing. Why this difficulty? It appears to relate to the fact that these two events—creation and production—occur in widely separated worlds.

Design engineers work in a controlled environment. Their highly trained and motivated technicians can all read, write, reason, and understand the mathematics of engineering. The equipment used to make a prototype is, more often than not, state of the art, well maintained, and calibrated. Working conditions, while not always up to operating-room standards, are invariably better than those on the shop floor. Achievement of test specifications with adjustment and fine tuning (the "tweak-and-peak twins")—a normal way of life with design engineers—assures success in that phase.

As we move to the plant floor, we hear "Good grief! They actually expect me to build that gadget? Those tolerances are so tight we don't have a micrometer that can even measure that close. And these milling machines! Come on, you have to be kidding! And personnel?"

"Well, do the best you can, Joe. I have another project to get hot on."

And Joe does the best his experience, expertise, and equipment will permit, but it doesn't result in what the customer wanted—and was assured you could deliver.

On a trip to Japan, I asked two companies how they handled this problem. Sadao Fujii, a quality engineer with Fujitsu Limited, confided that they assign some of their most promising young engineers to production for two or three years. During that period, these engineers receive a solid understanding of the real world of production. They learn that production-line workers seldom have the motivation or technical expertise of development personnel, that conditions are far less controlled, and that supervisor-worker communications are often inadequate.

The second firm, Ishikawa Jima-Harima Industries Company, has another practical approach. "We make the design engineers responsible for the product until it has achieved a cost-effective production level," says Kazuo Ishida, deputy general manager, aero-engine and space operations. This is certainly likely to cause some serious thought and to improve communications between the lab and production floor.

At least some U.S. firms seem to be catching on. At Texas Instruments' Trinity Mills facility, one of the production group supervisors, when asked what he had done before his current assignment, confessed he had been in design. What has the experience taught him? "These things are one hell of a lot easier to design than to build." There is little doubt that, when he returns to design, he—and the company—will be much better for the experience. Meanwhile, his time in production will be invaluable in product transition from design.

## LOW OPINION OF WORKERS' CAPABILITIES

One of my greatest disappointments in visiting American industry is the low opinion management appears to have of the workers' ability to compete with the Japanese in the realm of quality.

"Our people can never achieve the success the Japanese have in the field of quality. The cultural differences, the Japanese proclivity for detail, and their acceptance of regimentation and group orientation give them an advantage with which we can't compete. The Japanese workers' respect for authority, their willingness to accept less for their labor, the lack of union interference . . ."

It is true that the Japanese, in most cases, are culturally conditioned to be more attentive to detail. However, in studying the plan of Fujitsu's Institute of Management Training, one sees that this attention to detail is, for the most part, taught, not inherited. Flower and tea ceremonies, judo, and karate are all great detail disciplines.

The Japanese have unions—company unions rather than trade unions—but, nevertheless, bargaining units. As for ease of regimentation: Visit a U.S. Navy boot camp sometime and see how easily an off-the-street, do-your-own-thing dropout can be transformed into a spit-and-polish, precision-perfect example of enviable man- or womanhood. How is this achieved? Quite simply by requiring them to conform if they desire to continue. The same thing can be achieved with American workers.

Honda's Maryville, Ohio, plant reinforces this conclusion. At this plant, where the production force and majority of the supervisory force consist of U.S. men and women, the uniformed discipline equals that in Japanese plants—as do the quality standards. The Japanese general manager of the Maryville plant expects to exceed the quality achieved by Accords produced in his homeland, and it seems likely he will. Sony proved that this is possible when one line produced defect-free TVs for 200 continuous days in its San Diego plant. This record eclipses the best record Japanese workers have achieved.

So if cultural differences aren't the problem, what is? The problem is that management undersells American workers on what they can do or how *good* they really are. There are no finer workers in the world than American workers—once they are *told* what is expected of them and then held accountable for achieving it. They are not laissez-faire workers. Left to their own desires and their independent natures, for the most part, they do no more than a jumper being trained for a steeplechase. If you allow the horse to hurdle only those bars it easily clears on the first try, be assured it will never go any higher. Let the horse knock down the bars, but keep urging it to try harder by raising the bars and, if it has the potential to excel, it will!

### Union Considerations

Unions have contributed positively to the work force since their rise to power in our industrialized society, but, as Lord Acton so succinctly stated, "Power corrupts and absolute power corrupts absolutely." Today, unions often have a poor image among management and the public, the result of occasional infiltration of our labor unions by criminal elements, plus the periodic rise to power of corrupt leaders (or the corruption of those who have risen to power). Another reason has been an insistence on ever-increasing wages and fringe benefits, the costs of which are passed on to the consumer, who is often stuck with a fixed income.

Nevertheless, the insistence by management that unions per se are responsible for poor quality is invalid. Unions have provided a single voice for the most important factor in manufacturing—the production force. The two basic curses of U.S. trade unions are greed and a refusal to accept the fundamental economic premise that higher quality is the only path to increased productivity and improved competitiveness in the marketplace, and that these, in turn, are the only means of supporting higher reward.

Unions in Japan, recognizing these facts, have supported quality rather than assuming that the quality drive is just another management ploy to increase profits by exploiting labor. In a 1983 interview, Noriyuki Sugihara, elected head of the company union at Hewlett-Packard's Yokogawa plant in Hichioji-Shi, Japan, explained,

> We recognize that there are two approaches to improving labor's best interests. The first is to insist on a bigger share of the profits. This is valid to only a very limited degree. Since management supplies the capital, one of the two basic ingredients in production, they require and deserve a fair return on investment and effort. Repeated demands by labor for a larger share soon discourage investors and management alike, and result in factory closure and job losses for labor. [Our steel and auto industries lend truth to this statement with the proliferation of silent plants now in evidence.]
>
> The second approach is to improve productivity. Automatically our share becomes larger. You see, we believe in the theory that, rather than demanding a larger slice of the pie, we all benefit when we work together to produce a larger pie.

This approach has worked in Japan, and it can work in the United States. In fact, recent concessions made by both the auto and transportation unions lead one to believe that the philosophy is already being acknowledged by our own union leadership. Such team spirit can be easily extinguished when top management fails to accept a similar reduction in their inflated earnings and perks.

## Work Standards

What are your work standards? Have you established any? While some quality experts deny the need for quantified work standards, I believe they are valid. Taken in a vacuum, they are inadequate and destined to failure. But, taken in the context of factors we have already discussed, work standards not only set goals, but also convey to your most important resource—your people—what you expect of them.

## Training As a Condition

Both chapters 1 and 11 discuss training, so I'll not go into detail here, except to say it is a critical factor in the quality equation. You *assume* the qualification of your production personnel at your own peril. Few people seeking employment will confess that they lack any skill you desire and, in periods of high unemployment, this is not unexpected. Desired skill levels are better assured by hiring untrained persons and teaching them your production methods. But to let people run amuck on your production line without training or company-oriented certification is akin to jumping off the Golden Gate Bridge under the delusion that you're lighter than air.

## IS YOUR GOAL ZERO DEFECTS?

What should the ultimate goal be? Zero defects—and nothing less. One of the great proponents of the zero-defect approach is Philip B. Crosby, chairman of the board and CEO of the Quality College. Crosby's philosophy is that you don't hire or pay people to make defective products or to provide unsatisfactory services. If you agree with Crosby, you use zero defects as a criterion for employment. Why not establish "Do it right the first time" as a company production philosophy?

A number of years ago, the quality buzzwords were *zero defects*. After all, argued Crosby, "do we ever hire anyone to do a job incorrectly?" The answer to that question is, of course not! We hire them to do it right, and *right* the *first time*. However, statistics argue that there is variability in everything, no two things are exactly alike. Who then can define perfection? Is there anything that is defect free? My problem with the zero-defect philosophy is that it obviates the "threat role" played by our competitors. While we are dedicating our efforts to creating a defect-free product, our competitors are searching for ways to improve their products so that they have more to offer to a dynamic market.

Case in point. At the end of World War II, the United States, as has been pointed out in Howard K. Smith's perceptive foreword, ended with the only completely intact industrial system. How was a badly mauled Japan to compete with an industrial giant of unlimited land and resources such as this country?

Dr. Deming suggested that statistical quality control (SQC) would assist Japan in producing products more competitive by reason of their quality, while at the same time lower production costs by virtue of reducing the amount of scrap and rework they had to absorb as overhead. This made sense to the Japanese, who then went a step further. Let's design *innovatively* to woo the customer with the *practicality* of our product, that is, we design with *them* in mind. A check under the hood and on the dashboard of a

Japanese-designed car will confirm what I have described. It extends to optics, electronics, watches—you name it. Dr. Deming, the dean of American quality practitioners, terms it simply "constant improvement," with the customer in mind, naturally. Dr. J. M. Juran, one of America's leading quality authorities, has observed that many U.S. industries have accepted a 15 percent scrap rate as normal. Japan's is about 1 percent.[4]

In 1979, when Thomas J. Murrin was president of the Westinghouse Public Systems unit, that company began a corporate-wide, top-priority emphasis on productivity improvement—not a one-shot effort, but a way-of-life change throughout the corporation.[5] By studying successful Japanese industries, Westinghouse learned that quality begets productivity. The company's goal was to improve productivity—based on annual increases in constant-dollar value added per employee—by 6 percent per year. In the first three years of that program, Public Systems, including its defense group, achieved greater than a 7 percent annual productivity increase. Murrin said, "Now we're striving to get to 10 percent per year. A 7 percent improvement rate would double our output every 10 years, and a 10 percent rate would do this in about seven years."

The common complaint about zero defects as a quality policy is that it is unachievable. After all, as humans we are imperfect, and zero defects implies perfection. Here is what William F. Gibbs, designer of the S.S. *America*, has to say about perfection: "Perfection is an extremely hard taskmaster. . . . In the arts and sciences, it does not come easily. It comes hard. To get perfection, you have to demand perfection, and the people who demand perfection are rarely popular . . . and when it comes to perfection, I am implacable."

Man is imperfect, no question. But, if his goal in life or industry is less than perfection, he will achieve far less. Life should be a continuing search for improvement. This is what quality is all about: our search for excellence in our work and in our relationships with family and co-workers, all those aspects that we associate with quality of life. For those who feel that any nation has cornered the market on effort or the work ethic, or who believe the United States should take a back seat to anyone in the area of initiative or innovation, I'd like to remind them of the special edge this nation possesses.

We are uniquely blessed as a nation that has prided itself on being the melting pot. Our heterogeneous population is composed of people who, from the arrival of the Pilgrims, sought refuge in this land to escape oppression and avail themselves of the unlimited opportunities: a country rich in land and resources and having a temperate climate that allows people the freedom to excel. Even the convicts who settled Georgia emigrated to get that second chance. Today, our land welcomes refugees from the Middle East, Southeast Asia, South and Central America, Europe, the former USSR, and Africa—people who are not afraid to work and contribute to the greatness of our society.

Regrettably, the media often find it more newsworthy to focus on the sordid, rebellious, negative minority, whose only chance of immortality is to make headlines in protest or to engage in irrational behavior. Fortunately, the majority of our nation consists of people willing, able, and ready to work, produce, and excel. They need only leadership and goals to galvanize them into a cohesive machine that won't accept failure.

It is my belief that management has failed to provide the caliber of leadership and guidance that considers the unions, supplier control, and worker motivation as challenges, instead of someone else's concern. If affluence has demotivated our working population, we need only to return to a policy of pay commensurate with productivity. We need to set goals and require accountability from all.

## PROCESS CONTROL

Regrettably, during this period of exploding technology, we find the quality control function still using horse-and-buggy techniques. Specifically, many industries continue to pursue a quality control program based on final inspection.

What are the user benefits of final inspection as the essence of a quality control program? Printed circuit boards or integrated circuits that don't meet test criteria are either tossed into the scrap pile or sent back for rework. Production chiefs in the semiconductor business report that, at times, the scrap rate can tote up to 80 percent on new and exotic designs.

When defective product is scrapped, the entire investment—materials, labor, manufacturing facilities—is lost. The only possible value of this scrap is that, with a sound analysis program, it can pinpoint design deficiencies. Meanwhile, the rework pile will increase the cost of production by a factor of three: initial production; the rework effort that requires personalized repair and will, therefore, invariably require an effort greater than the original production-line investment; and the product that will not be made due to the production effort required by rework.

At a modest transceiver assembly plant in southern Florida, 50 of the 250 production people were engaged in rework. The solution, simple and certainly not new, is process control. This approach analyzes the manufacturing process and determines where glitches are most likely to occur. Statistical process control represents a major contribution at this point, since it is both data factual and sensitive.

Who should be responsible for doing process control checks? I suggest it should be production personnel. Those who produce must accept the responsibility for the quality of their efforts and be held accountable for it. Quality personnel perform the invaluable task of auditing production's efforts, reviewing process control procedures, collecting and analyzing data, suggesting corrective action upon evaluation of failure analysis, and then, most importantly, following up to ensure corrective action has been taken.

The foregoing should not be interpreted to mean that limited final inspection is unnecessary. First-article inspection is essential. This tells you if you have achieved your customers' desires and if the product fills your customers' needs. It is essential at this point to expeditiously implement any required corrective action. Thereafter, audits to ensure that the process is still in control should be adequate.

### Material and Component Availability

One of the characteristics of the American defense industry today is that very few, if any, of the larger prime contractors are anything more than integration or assembly plants. This introduces one of the really tough aspects of process control—supplier quality assurance.

And who is responsible for vendor quality? "Elementary," you may say. "The supplier, of course."

Wrong. Whose name goes on the end item—yours or the supplier's?

"Why, mine, but . . ."

No buts. Buyers give not one hoot that ABC and XYZ supplied everything but the casing. They see the proud name of LMO Company on that assembled engine case and that's the name on the delivery invoice. Now who do you think is responsible?

Ultimately, the prime contractor is responsible. However, that company must never allow the supplier to take advantage of that fact by delegating all responsibility for quality to the prime contractor. At one point in our country's history—the period during which we like to brag that "a man's word was as good as his bond"—certification by the vendor that the quality had been "built in" might have been taken at face value. Nowadays, the safest route is to act as if you're from Missouri and require objective evidence that the supplier can deliver quality on schedule.

Toyota has become famous for its just-in-time inventory receiving. Instead of having large warehouses for an extensive inventory with the attendant operating cost and capital investment, Toyota requires room for only two hours of inventory. At Sony's Ichinomiya plant, a Sony TV or VCR rolls off the line every six seconds. Does this require a large inventory of parts?

"No," says Kinnosuke Ikeda, manager, administrative affairs. "Every 90 minutes trucks from our suppliers roll up and disgorge the components we need; we let them keep the inventory for us." But, of even greater importance, the suppliers know that for Sony to produce made-right-the-first-time TVs and VCRs, it needs quality parts. Moreover, the suppliers' futures as Sony suppliers depend on their delivery of just that.

Yamazaki MAZAK Co., Ltd., in Oguchi, Niwa-Gun, has a unique approach to vendor control. When I visited Yamazaki, I noted a tote board laden with kanji-covered shingles hung in a prominent spot in the receiving area. "That's our scoreboard," explained Kazuo Nishimura, international marketing manager. "To get on the top level, a supplier must have a 95 percent or better yield of no-defect delivery. And to get on the second level, a supplier must have a 92 percent or better."

There is no third level. "Suppliers in the lower level are always competing for the top level, knowing that if Yamazaki has to cut back, the first to go will be the second-tier suppliers," Nishimura says. This makes the suppliers compete for Yamazaki's business, with the winning edge being quality.


## MARKETING CONSTRAINTS

How can marketing detract from quality? By overselling the product to the customer. Oversell can occur in slick "brochuresmanship" that describes or implies product characteristics beyond the state of the art or beyond the firm's capability to manufacture. A second oversell is the unrealistic delivery schedule. At times this may be at the insistence of the buyer—at other times, the suggestion of the marketer anxious to beat out the competition. Be aware of the negative impact this has on quality in either case. In the first situation, the buyer may schedule a production line start-up or new product introduction based on promised delivery date. This can lead to suits and countersuits. Certainly it will lead to ill will and, in all probability, a lost customer. Where the described production capability does not exist, it can, at a minimum, raise doubts about the integrity of a sales force. Integrity is very much an issue in quality.

## MANAGEMENT COMMITMENT

One of the most important elements of the complex makeup of quality is management commitment. It is important for two basic reasons. First, management sets the quality policy, and second, management controls the resources.

### Quality Policy
It is dismaying to discover old-line, well-respected, state-of-the-art companies that either have no quality policy, or have established one only very recently. They have established policies for working hours, sick leave, vacation pay, retirement, and incentive benefits, but have not considered quality sufficiently important, until recently, to require a published policy.

What should the policy say and who should get it? Appendix D has some samples, but basically it should be brief enough to attract interest, but adequate to cover the pertinent aspects of how management feels about quality. There are policy statements that are as brief as two sentences and others that run six typewritten pages. The former is preferable. Too often, the latter gives the feeling that it is management's attempt to impress stockholders or customers. The policy should really exist to explain concisely and understandably the degree of attention to quality that management desires, and to assign responsibility for its achievement.

Take note: Once a quality policy exists, don't try to short-circuit it because certain customers want an early delivery and are willing to sign any kind of waiver to get it. This is a two-edged sword. Your workers will now know you have exceptions, following company quality policy only when convenient, and the customers may only be willing to forgo quality until they take delivery and find that the product doesn't fulfill either their own or their customers' expectations. Military procurement personnel can cite numerous examples of the truth of this statement.

### Resource Control
The second critical issue, which is solely the prerogative of top management, is control of resources: Capital investment that will improve quality, expensive

training effort, and creation of new areas of corporate expenditure are all decisions made by top management.

As Alvin Gunneson, CEO of the Gunneson Group, International, is wont to say, "I'm not interested in management support; I'm interested, as a quality manager, in participation!" This implies understanding of who is ultimately responsible for quality (the CEO) and how it is achieved (the result of an all-hands effort).

Much of the problem in the area of quality today, I believe, stems from inability of the quality community to effectively communicate with CEOs and COOs. The issue, I believe, is that they do not understand the complexity of the quality issue, its importance to survival and success, and the essentiality of their active participation in the concept.

## SIMPLY COMPLEX

What, then, is quality? It is a simple idea that becomes extremely complex when we try to put it in practice. Quality is as simple as the idea of making it right the first time, and as complex as the host of actions required to conceive, design, make, sell, and service any product.

In the final analysis, it is profit to the producer, value to the buyer, and satisfaction to both: profit to the producer because concentration on quality has raised productivity and thus generated a better return on investment and sustained competitive advantage; value to the buyer because the focus on quality has assured customers that what they have purchased are products that will fit not only their needs, but provide them with the reliability that will keep them coming back, convinced that the producer has *their* best interests in mind.

While this preoccupation with quality has a real-time payoff, of far greater value is the long-range ramification of top management's active participation in the enhancement of this nation's quality reputation and its ability to compete domestically with imports and recapture foreign markets once ours. This, in the final analysis, is how our economic problems will be solved.

## NOTES

1. Robert M. Pirsig, *Zen and the Art of Motorcycle Maintenance* (New York: Bantam Books, 1974).

2. *American Heritage Dictionary*, 2d College Edition (Boston: Houghton Mifflin, 1982), 1013.

3. Major General A. G. Rogers (USAF), "Product User," National Security Industrial Quality Conference, Hunt Valley, Md., October 20, 1982.

4. Speech by J. M. Juran at Bottom-Line Conference sponsored by Defense Logistics Agency, Washington, D.C., at Fort McNair, May 13, 1982.

5. Speech by Thomas J. Murrin at Bottom-Line Conference sponsored by Defense Logistics Agency, Washington, D.C., at Fort McNair, May 13, 1982.

# 3 WHO IS RESPONSIBLE?

## OBSERVED MISCONCEPTIONS

Ask the senior person in almost any company who is responsible for quality in the company. As if by reflex, the CEO, COO, general manager, or other senior manager will point to the quality manager. Among defense contractors, an alternative is to point at the Defense Contract Administration Service quality assurance representative (DCASQAR). "That's interesting," you might respond. "In what section of production or design is that person assigned? Is he or she a welder, lathe operator, engineer, drafter, or what?"

"Why, none of those. That's my quality manager," will come the puzzled reply.

How can quality managers possibly be responsible for quality when they don't *make* anything? With the possible exceptions of inspections, charts, statistical reports, and perhaps slogans, the entire quality function produces nothing.

A second answer, received on rare occasions, is, "I am responsible for quality." That is a candid admission. In the final analysis, the top dog *is* responsible for quality. However, as we will see in this chapter, quality is *not* a one-person show.

Some companies already recognize that fact. At a visit to Gould Defense Electronic Division in Glen Burnie, Maryland, I asked the question, "How many of you are in quality?" The unanimous, unprompted response: "We all are." Gould employees made the point.

**Top Management's Responsibilities**

*Attention to Detail.*    Top managers as a rule are not detail oriented. Marketing and financial strategy are key to the important decisions they must consider. Middle management and production are more likely to be responsible for details. Don't you believe that a top manager who is unfamiliar with essential details of his business won't find him or herself stranded on a lee shore at some point in their career, wondering what happened.

The late Admiral Hyman G. Rickover, USN (Ret), father of nuclear propulsion in the U.S. Navy and certainly a legend in his own lifetime, said this about detail *and* top management: "The man in charge must concern himself with details. If *he* does not consider them important, neither will his subordinates. Most managers would rather focus on lofty policy issue matters. But, when details are ignored, the project fails. To maintain proper control, one must have simple and direct means to find out what is going on. There are many ways of doing this; all involve drudgery."

Rickover's words have a definite message for managers who aspire to success. Know what is going on and you will be much better prepared to plan, anticipate, act, and react as the situation dictates. By knowing what is going on, you can become master of your fate, captain of your ship, as it were.

*Being Visible.*    This knowledge of what is going on must extend to knowing, and showing concern for, your people, and it must be concern that is more solid than fancy words and PR about how people-oriented the XYZ Company is. Demonstrate how people-oriented you are by visiting workers on the shop floor, in the cafeteria, and at company athletic events. Know your plants and people. Is that too much to ask? Are you too busy to get out and see what's going on? A glimpse of the president or CEO walking through the plant, asking questions and showing interest, has a value in boosted morale that no amount of money can buy.

"Why, the boss is a real person. Look how short/tall, attractive/homely, impressive/plain looking. Asked me my name. Even asked me to explain what I was doing, how long I'd been with the company, what I thought of working conditions. Shook hands with me, too." These are the spirit-boosting comments you will invariably hear when you take the trouble to get out to see and be seen by people most responsible for your success as a CEO or COO.

*Sales Ability.*    A successful top manager must also be a super salesperson. It's obvious you had those qualities on the day you drove into corporate headquarters and parked in the slot marked "President."

Now, however, you have reached a point where you must sell yourself not only to your superiors, but also to your peers and subordinates. Let's discuss the two new breeds of superiors you must sell: they are the board of directors—and you will get to know them intimately—and the stockholders, that faceless group who, at each year's stockholders' meeting, can ask all sorts of interesting and embarrassing questions. How are you going to answer their questions about deferred dividends or reverses in stock prices? U.S. management, in general, has done little to sell the idea of long-range growth and company stability for the future. Rather, preoccupation with short-term growth, acquisition, and significant ROI have been the yardstick by which CEOs and COOs are measured. This false philosophy will have to be altered if we are to survive in the international market.

Plant modernization, increased investment in research and development, and sounder wage and benefit guidelines based on production are important arrangement decisions. They are essential if the ship of industry is to catch the freshening breeze of innovative management and long-range planning to lift it out of the doldrums and put it on a competitive course for the market.

How do you sell this to stockholders and a board of directors? "The most challenging aspect of management," replies Gen. Shigeto Nagano, JSDF (Ret), executive vice president of Fujitsu System Integration Laboratories, "is to convince our stockholders that our management goals are to ensure a continued growth of their investment, and to provide a strength and stability for Fujitsu that will relieve them of concern about the future. It is not easy, but it is essential."[1]

Just as top management at times sells the U.S. worker short regarding its capabilities, we also sell the stockholders and directors short on their ability to understand and accept the logic of growth and stability vs. gimmickry and short-range gain. Needless to say, you must have a long-range plan that *produces*, or you will lose not only the stockholders' support for a long-range strategy, but your position as ruler of the corporate hill.

*Corporate Expansion.*  Corporate subsumption of companies often leads the parent cormpany into unfamiliar manufacturing areas. One might argue that, since the previous owners are present to provide continuity in management, there should not be a ripple in the new corporate configuration. This overlooks the degree of interest ownership normally provides vis-a-vis the former owner's current role of just being an employee. For top management to have the responsibility for making major product-line decisions in areas of ignorance can often spell disaster. One must understand the unique complexity of the market for one's product line. The auto industry is an example of management's ignorance or insensitivity to the market. This ignorance resulted in a Titanic-like disaster. Some may argue that knowing the product is unimportant at the top level—that knowledge of law or finance is more important. But consider the number of businesses going belly up during the late 1980s and early 1990s. It may well be that this epidemic is at least in part the predictable result of inadequate knowledge of market and quality.

### Responsibilities of the Quality Manager

If quality managers (vice president, directors, and so on) are not responsible for quality, then what are they responsible for? Quality managers serve many important functions. They should, above all else, understand the process by which products are manufactured so that they can evaluate the potential effectiveness of proposed quality control assurance procedures. This means that they should be a part of the design/development operation, to help determine whether the product can survive the transition from lab to production line.

Quality managers should ensure that production engineers are part of this review. In coordination with the production boss, they should determine who will perform the in-process measurements. If production accepts this responsibility—which is rightfully theirs—then the quality function should audit the results. Quality should also be responsible for collecting and analyzing data on quality improvement or deterioration, and for publishing this information for managers and workers in the design and production areas. As the result of statistical analysis, those functions should support the production boss in recommending new equipment or facilities that will improve quality to top management.

Evaluating, routing, and following up on failure analysis and corrective action should be key aspects of quality's job—it is the only way to prevent the same problems from arising again and again.

Customer product satisfaction must also be of prime concern to quality. This can be accomplished through personal interaction with customers, survey questionnaires, customer orientation conferences and tours, and other means.

### Government Representative's Responsibility

If you are a defense contractor, you will probably have a DCASQAR in your facilities, either as a resident, nonresident, or Defense Contract Administration Service plant representative officer (DCASPRO). The resident is *just* that and may have significant staff, depending on plant, contract size, and product complexity. If you are a smaller plant or are dealing with a smaller, less-complex contract, it's more likely you'll work with a nonresident government representative. (Nonresident governmental quality people are each assigned approximately three contractors.) In any case, the quality representative will not only be responsible for monitoring quality assurance for your military or government customers, but may cover several other plants with defense contracts.

A very large plant with a high-dollar-value contract or high-visibility product, such as the external fuel tank for the space shuttle, may be assigned a DCASPRO. The responsibilities of the DCASPRO include contract administration and property disposal personnel. In remote locations, you may often have an officer-in-charge organization, which is larger than a residency but smaller than a DCASPRO.

These people are responsible for the customers' best interests. The purchasing or procurement contract officer—for the army, navy, air force, post office, NASA, or the Department of Energy—writes or lets the contracts, but the Defense Contract Administration Service (DCAS) has full responsibility for administering them.

In addition, DCAS may be charged to do a preaward survey to determine the capability of a contractor to fulfill the terms of the contract, not only from a facilities standpoint, but also from financial, management, and engineering standpoints. The procurement contract officer does not have to accept this recommendation and, sometimes, either because of a paucity of bidders or a visceral hunch, will award contrary to the DCAS recommendation. In addition, DCAS may institute postaward conferences to ensure that contractors (particularly new ones) fully understand what is expected of them.

Administering a contract includes a close review to ensure that the contract clearly states what customers want and the level of quality they expect for their money. The most stringent quality requirements are found in contracts for nuclear power propulsion plant system components. Level one subsafe products are the next most stringent. MIL-Q-9858A is the most stringent nonspecial products requirement. It insists on complete documentation of the quality control system and a report on all elements that contribute to cost of quality—an onerous and misleading label, since the cost is really caused by nonconformance, not by quality data.

Another standard, MIL-I-45208A, is less demanding. It implicitly relies more on inspection than process control. Less demanding still is standard Form 32, which assumes QC to be the responsibility of the contractor. As a result, there is no formalized procedure specified in the contract.

The DCASQAR is responsible for reviewing the contractor's quality control system to see if it will meet the customer's quality desires. First-article inspection, if called for by contract, spot checks to ensure that the quality process is controlled, and end-item spot checks supplement the front-end verification of vendor components or base materials. The representative's signature does three things: It confirms acceptability of material to the contractor, signals the paying office to write a check, and assures the customer that the product is as specified in the contract.

As is readily apparent, the DCASQAR, while not responsible for quality, is responsible for seeing that products failing to meet customer specs are not shipped. A key person in the quality equation, the DCASQAR must never be intimidated by contractor or customer.

There is always the possibility of intimidation by contractors who have a quality or cash flow problem, or who feel that military specs are not binding on a company that successfully supplies similar products to the private sector. Customers can also be very intimidating when pushed by schedule or budget windows, and may press the DCASQAR to accept the finished product on waivers. If the product was initially overspecified and performs satisfactorily despite noncompliance, the contractor and the quality representative may escape unscathed. But if the product fails as has occurred in the past (and particularly if it draws media attention), the DCASQAR and the contractor who waived specs may be in for a pounding.

Waivers and material review board actions are both signals that specifications have not been met and, although the customer may approve a discrepancy, the supplier ships with the risk of customer dissatisfaction. If the customer is genuinely happy, the supplier should consider an engineering change proposal to bring the specs into accord with the new standard inadvertently created.

Failure to heed DCASQAR counsel concerning procedure or product quality may inspire the DCASQAR to activate corrective action methods ranging from a verbal suggestion to withdrawal of the DCASQAR's product quality assurance activities from the contractor's plant. Then, unless the customer will accept the product without a DCASQAR signature indicating satisfactory quality assurance, the contractor may suddenly come down with a severe case of cash flow anemia. The DCASQAR may also call attention to the supplier's quality problems and advise the customer to investigate.

Government representatives should be considered members of the quality team that is looking out for the best interests of the contractor—a means of enabling the contractor to continue delivering products to customers who do not normally experience the economic fluctuations of the private sector. These government representatives also consider the interests of taxpayers, who are increasingly burdened by deeper incursions into their pocketbooks. DCASQARs must be allowed to be objective outsiders who enjoy a nonadversarial relationship—if they are to be able to help with contractor quality problems and with keeping customer relationships on an even keel.

### Prime Contractor's Quality Rep
If you are a subcontractor, as most manufacturers now are with the trend toward specialization, you may have a prime contractor quality rep assigned. The representative's function is to look after you and the prime contractor's best interests. To get rid of the rep, you will have to hone your manufacturing system to the fine point of being able to consistently ship defect-free products to the rep's employer. At that point, the prime contractor will have no alternative but to remove the company's rep from your plant, since that rep has obviously become an unnecessary expense for the company.

### Production's Responsibility
The lion's share of responsibility for quality occurs on the production line, but an "undoable" design can doom quality, as can equipment incapable of holding required tolerances. Purchasing inferior materials or components can also negatively affect production. The low bidder whose bid is based on poor quality can turn out to be the biggest drain on profits or the main cause of cost overruns.

The shipping department, too, can thwart production's best attempts to produce a quality product by damaging the finish, causing misalignment, poor packaging, or just not following the customer's contract instructions. If the customer, for instance, has specified one valve per box and the shipping department packs two, quality has not been delivered. Customers can seem unreasonably demanding at times, but remember, they are your raison d'être.[2] While it is perfectly logical for the government to want to be good stewards of public funds, low bid is not necessarily the way to do so. Often, unqualified manufacturers, or even brokers who have no facilities, will bid a job low and then shop for someone to build it for them. This means that, for either to survive, they have to pare everything to the bone. Normally, this will include quality, and the government ends up with junk. No procurement contract officer knowingly awards a contract to an unqualified bidder, but sometimes there is insufficient time to investigate and sometimes political pressures are brought to bear. In such cases, the quality system takes the crunch.

## WHEN EVERYONE'S RESPONSIBLE, IS ANYONE RESPONSIBLE?

If everyone has a piece of the quality pie, on whom do you pin the tail when quality sours? President Truman's oft-quoted desk sign, "The Buck Stops Here," has been misinterpreted to mean that no one below the top has sufficient responsibility to be held accountable. That kind of thinking can be disastrous. If a general manager, through lack of attention to detail and counsel, steers the corporation into an extreme situation, he or she should be fired—not transferred to corporate headquarters to cool off or retire gracefully. If the production chief cannot produce a quality product despite a debugged design and on-spec materials, then the production chief—not the quality chief—should be pink slipped. If the maintenance personnel cannot maintain equipment and the custodial division cannot keep the working area free of debris, their replacement is reasonable. These removals should not be done without counseling or warning, but all parties must recognize that the concept of accountability includes this unpleasant repercussion. A laissez-faire approach to accountability in both the private and public sectors regrettably has oftimes created the illusion that there is no accountability for anything up to and including murder in our society.

### Blue vs. White Collar

Deming attributes the bulk of quality errors to the system, and the system belongs to management.[3] Why then is it so popular to beat up on the blue-collar work force? Probably because white-collar workers are more adroit at passing the buck down than blue-collar workers are at passing it up. If the product is out of tolerance, it would be fairly easy to trace down the errant artificer who has a controlling contribution to that process.

Design has remained aloof and remote from the area where the chips and sparks fall. Designers often consider their responsibility ended once the design has been committed to hard copy. Similarly, management has always excused environments that militate against quality.

"Automation? Too expensive and business too slow. Update of machinery? No. The board of directors will never sanction it. Training? I learned my trade through on-the-job training. Insufficient time to develop and produce? Okay, design and production, work it out. We need this contract. Have quality report directly to the general manager? Why, if I do that, the next thing I know, the quality manager will be wanting more money." Those responses can devastate a quality program.

Marketing's attitude problems sound like this: "Visit a customer to see if he's satisfied with our product? Look, I have too much to do trying to sell our product. I can't spend time checking to see if anyone has any problems."

Or, "If we tell the customer we can't deliver in that time frame, we'll lose the order. Besides, the customer's not too fussy when we're late." Or, "I thought you production guys could do anything. I told the customer we could improve on the specs."

Deming's identification of management as the main cause of quality problems is due to its responsibility for all the significant decisions regarding resources, facilities, and engineering. To exempt these elements from accountability for quality is indeed mindless management.

When we speak of management (those mysterious forces who always seem to be pitted against our best interests), who do we mean? For our purposes, *management* is anyone who has authority to allocate or withhold resources and make policy decisions. Those two abilities identify management as the most important factor in industry's side of the house as far as quality is concerned.

### Loyalty

Loyalty, for the most part, has become rather passé in today's workaday world. People do not identify with the LMO Company to the degree they once did. This is because, in our mobile layoff-oriented, and recall-prone industrial world, workers move from one job to another as the opportunity presents itself. Japanese management marvels at our ability to exact *any* loyalty with on-off hiring policies dictated by market demand and economy.

The adversarial relationship that has characterized management-labor relations for so many years is another area that discourages company identity and loyalty, and that, in turn, does nothing to increase dedication to higher quality.

Recent actions on the part of the rank-and-file workers (voting unions out of plants or opposing their formation) demonstrate that workers are beginning to demand a greater concern for their best interests from union leaders. Arbitrary rejection of company wage packages, when the logic of the proposals is obvious, has aroused a tide of worker resentment as well as public sentiment against the unions' self-serving leadership. Conversely, failure of management to keep faith with labor after such a concession, by awarding top management huge bonuses, can be disastrous.

Recall the time when we thought the workers were the company. The return of such a feeling of identity and unity of purpose will have a salutary effect on quality, and the return of this identity factor is dependent on union leadership and corporate management that can demonstrate that they have workers' best interests at heart. Lifetime employment, willingness to compromise to promote the best interests of all concerned, willingness to go that extra mile, implementation of quality circles (discussed in chapter 12)—all these will convince workers that they are truly a part of the LMO Company and that their interests are best served by quality work that enhances productivity and permits them to *earn* what they are being paid.

## THE CUSTOMER'S ROLE

The customer, too, plays a vital role in the quality of the delivered product. His role begins with the writing of the contract. The contract should not leave much to a contractor's imagination. It is *insufficient* for the customer to know what he wants. He must also *communicate* his desires to the contractor.

Nor should specs of related items be scattered throughout the contract. Some customers feel that, if a spec is in there, it's the contractor's responsibility to ferret it out and comply. In contrast, the customer who is really interested in quality will work to eliminate anything that may give the contractor problems.

A case in point: A customer's receiving department was complaining that 99 percent of the products received were not packaged correctly. What could possibly account for that remarkable level of nonconformance? The desired packaging was specified in the contract, but bureaucratese and legalese had so garbled the instructions that it took a professional contracting officer a couple of hours to unscramble it. Consider the poor bicycle shop, with limited talent, trying to piece it all together. Legally, the customer in this case was clear, but the unclear specs were tantamount to no specs when it came to assuring the desired quality.

Even the U.S. Navy can be, at times, a customer who places unreasonable demands on contractors. Concerned with keeping ahead of our military foes, the navy understandably wants the latest that technology has to offer, and they want it today. A senior military spokesman, a fleet commander, put it this way: "The navy should be more patient by not insisting on production of a weapon before it is mature. We need a working, reliable system when it gets there."[4] As the saying in Washington goes, "If you want it bad, you get it bad."

### Standardized Contract Form

Another way the customer hinders quality and distresses contractors is by using nonstandard contract forms. This is particularly true of military contracts. Each service—yes, each procurement contract office—may have its own contract format. To a small contractor with limited legal expertise and limited staff, this can pose a problem. It becomes difficult to determine whether all the wheat in a chaff-filled contract has been successfully gleaned.

Part of the problem is the varying degree of expertise and experience that government quality assurance representatives (QARs) possess. Fortunately, many of their basic training courses have recently been revised, and several new courses have been instituted. As more QARs complete these courses, inspection—and contracts—should become more standardized.

### Performance Expectations

When specs call for precise tolerance or documentation and then these specs are waived to get delivery, the contractor questions whether the customers really know what they want. The contractor wonders the same thing when the customers specify an item that is clearly beyond the state of the art. "But unless we push the state of the art, we will never know what is possible," you might argue. That may be true in basic research or in research and development projects, but when the item in question is truly meant to be produced and delivered to a consumer with immediate needs, realism—not reaching—is what specs should reflect.

The point here is for the customer: If you are interested in quality, spell out what you want and then demand it. If it's impossible to produce, acknowledge this and reduce the spec, but avoid waivers. They *desensitize* the contractor and make a mockery of your real needs.

Much customer-contractor confusion can be eliminated by improved communications. Candid admission of confusion early on may save a heap of embarrassment later. Is it better to be thought dull or found stupid?

## THE FOUNDATION

But where is the first brick, rebar, and mortar of quality laid? I suggest it's in the home. Parents who lack the foresight or intellect to teach children responsibility for their actions, those who fail to follow up when children disobey or fail to complete assigned tasks (chores or school work), are planting the seeds of nonconformance. This is where phrases and attitudes like "good enough" or "good enough for government work" are conceived. The foundations of character are "poured" in the home. Schools, at times, can correct poor foundations, but don't count on it. If you question some other institutions' concern about your progeny's character, ensure that you take the time to do the foundation work yourself.

And what does this foundation laying have to do with quality? Almost everything. It's exemplified by parents who are interested enough in their children's futures to commend them for a job well done and counsel them on poor effort. It's a constant example of best effort by parents and relatives in all that they do. It's honesty lived in the home. It's personal habits of hanging up clothes, putting away tools, and keeping the house clean. Trivial as all this may seem, it sets the background for habits that, later in life, will identify and separate a quality-oriented person from one whose basic training has taught him to believe that getting by is adequate and that the 110 percent philosophy of former football coach, the late George Allen, is pure eyewash.

Just as quality is the product of a number of people, so is nonconformance. Developing a quality worker is a lifelong process; reorienting a worker who has never been taught or forced to care is no overnight task, regardless of the method used. But bear in mind, identification and understanding of the problem are the first giant steps toward correcting them.

### Academe

Ever since publication of the presidential panel's study on the quality of education in the United States, *A Nation at Risk*,[5] in 1983, America has become acutely aware of the fact that education in this country has been far from successful. Can we conclude that this situation has affected quality?

Most in the quality community would vote a resounding Yes! Education is the second rung in the development of a quality philosophy. It is in this environment that our future managers, engineers, computer programmers, lathe and machine operators learn to read and reason, multiply, divide, and understand equations and statistics. This is in primary and secondary schools.

In college, they learn how to think and reach decisions using a logical thought process. Regrettably, it appears we missed the boat at the readin', writin', and 'rithmetic stage. There is no way a person can be a quality craftsperson if he or she cannot read blueprints and machinery procedures—not in today's complex technology.

In addition to failing in the basics, many schools have failed in the philosophical area—where students learn the basic Rs of responsibility—first, the essentials of responsibility and, second, who is responsible for what.

The failure of business schools to emphasize top management's role in the quality equation is also most disquieting. So is the number of engineering schools that focus their quality curricula on inspection techniques rather than on process control. It is hoped that the first light in the academic community, ignited by the Defense Logistics Agency's Bottom-Line Conferences in April of 1983 and 1984, has continued to burn brightly with the fuel from the Malcolm Baldrige National Quality Award (MBNQA) and brought about significant change in engineering and management curricula.

## COST OF CHANGE

The navy, over the past few years, has taken a great deal of heat over its significant cost overruns. To the uninitiated, these overruns seem unreasonable. Many, however, are not unreasonable at all, but are caused by our rapidly changing technology. Failure to take advantage of technological changes would be imprudent, but the contractor will hardly feel inclined to give the customer (the navy) a bargain price for changes that affect his or her schedule. Hence, the navy pays through the nose. Cost overruns caused by these product improvements are not the problem. The problems are the engineering changes that occur as a result of the customer's not having provided proper specs. One contractor reports that a certain customer made *over* 5000 changes or corrections during production. That is inexcusable. Customers aren't alone in their culpability on changes. Contractors' design sections are probably equally guilty.

How does an engineering change affect quality? Once production has begun, if the change is significant, it requires reproving the line from a quality standpoint. It also raises questions in production as to the capabilities of design engineering.

### Government-Furnished Equipment

With the rapid growth of technology in both product and production machinery, it is often difficult for a producer to acquire quality production equipment, particularly if the producer operates on a slim profit margin. It is therefore not unusual for the military to underwrite the cost of new equipment (which is then designated "government-furnished equipment"). The customer will benefit in quality and schedule from such an investment. Expecting too much from old equipment can be more costly, in the end, than replacement.

## NOTES

1. Interview with Shigeto Nagano, executive vice president, Fujitsu System Integration Laboratories, Tokyo, Japan, 1982.

2. Translated: reason for being.

3. W. Edwards Deming, *Quality, Productivity, and Competitive Position* (Cambridge, Mass.: MIT Press, 1982), 68.

4. Remarks by Adm. Sylvester R. Foley, Jr. (USN) at Bottom-Line Conference sponsored by Defense Logistics Agency, Washington, D.C., at Fort McNair, June 1, 1983.

5. *A Nation at Risk*, National Commission on Education Excellence (President Ronald Reagan's blue-ribbon panel) issued April 26, 1983.

# 4 COMMON MISCONCEPTIONS

There are many common misconceptions that relate to management, the relationship of government and industry, culture, prosperity, affluence, and mobility, all of which affect quality. In warfare, the basic principle of victory is to know your enemy. In the case of quality, anything that inhibits its achievement is to be considered the enemy.

## KNOWING THE ENEMY

### Updating Facilities

*Can do* is a wonderful characteristic. The Sea Bees used it to good advantage during World War II as they carved bases out of steaming jungles and built harbors from coral-rimmed beaches in the South Pacific. *Make do* is quite another thing. Many plants make do with outdated, outmoded, and, in some cases, only marginally operative equipment and facilities. This may be because plant management intends to wait for better times to make a capital investment that should have been made long ago.

Putting off modernization until you can afford it is somewhat like putting off marriage or family for the same reason. In most cases, marriage makes life richer and fuller and, when you finally take the plunge, you wonder why you waited. So it is with modernizing a plant. It requires faith in the future. What during this nuclear age doesn't? It also requires confidence that modernization will improve productivity and reduce cost through quality; this in turn makes you more competitive during this era of peace, which finds our major adversary's economy and political structure in shambles thus mandating a reduction in the U.S. DOD budget. Those unable to meet the new standards of quality, the guidelines for which have been established by the TQM directive issued by the DOD, plus failing to meet cost competition, will soon find themselves out of business as DOD contractors.

The Defense Department has an inventory of outdated machinery at the Defense Industrial Plant Equipment Center. The equipment dates from World War II and the Korean War and, since contractors can use this machinery on defense contracts by paying only a refurbishing charge (if it is necessary), many avail themselves of it. This equipment was adequate in its day, but, unlike French wine, it does not get better with age.

Usually, you can draw a direct correlation between equipment and quality. In some few cases, people make the difference. Their dedication and skill enable them to make silk purses with sows' ears. But in most cases the product falls short.

### Government Aid

Because several industrial giants have been revived by government bailouts, there is a popular misconception that government aid will restore vitality to U.S. industry. As the old adage goes, "There are three classes of people: those who watch things happen, those who make things happen, and those who wonder what happened." Those who wait for the U.S. government to rescue them will wonder what happened when they go under.

Just what is the government's responsibility to business and commerce? It is to provide a free society in which business can compete, grow, succeed, and expand to international markets. Do we want it to play a bigger role? If you want government financing, you can count on giving up a degree of independence and freedom in management. Already we are engulfed in a sea of paper which, in and of itself, causes some entrepreneurs to throw in the towel.

Maintenance of a free society in which people are able to work, express themselves, and live in a reasonable degree of security is primarily what we in industry should expect from government. We should expect our tax dollars to keep the sea lanes open for commerce and promote mutual trade relations in the international marketplace. But Santa Claus, Uncle Sam *ain't.*

Political connections may promote largess from the public treasury, but they don't solve the management problems that caused the need. Government subsidies to industry weaken initiative, the impulse to innovate, and the ingenuity of management to operate in a competitive arena, creating a need for continued support.

Governments have no source of money except from the people they govern. Government is a nonproducing but significant consumer of public productivity. To the extent that government provides us a free and just society with free market opportunities, it is worth the price, but subsidies create the appearance of supporting employment and commerce. In the final analysis, they can sound the death knell to any industry that depends on them. Our merchant marine is a classic example of wages outpacing productivity and encouraging noncompetitiveness. Many will argue that the former Soviet Union and other European and Far Eastern nations keep their merchant fleets alive with subsidy. This is true, and to the extent that our merchant fleet is an auxiliary of our navy, our subsidies may be justified. But, in general, subsidies ensure that a business will never be self-supportive or competitive.

**Protective Tariffs**

The protective-tariff game is a vicious cycle that ultimately creates a lose-lose situation. It makes regulated trade in foreign markets almost impossible. It places an artificial barrier to peace by precluding free travel and cultural exchange that help us to know our neighbors. It's a game that admits the other fellow can do something better or cheaper than we can.

Instead of putting up a fence, why not examine why our neighbor excels? This is precisely what the Japanese did, with General MacArthur's urging and assistance. They examined the reasons U.S. goods were considered desirable while their own were considered "cheap junk."

Learning quickly and foregoing pride (so expensive to maintain), they adopted our methods of statistical quality control, and automation, and are presently outdoing us at our own game. Slapping a tariff or quota on Japanese cars is not the way to take care of the problem. Possibly not even joint ventures (GMC–Toyota, for example) are the answer, unless we are willing to admit that the Japanese are better designers or are superior in production or management methods.

For at least the past decade, U.S. executives and managers have made pilgrimages to Japan, Korea, and China, as well as Europe, to discover the magic formula our competitors are using to achieve entry to and, in some cases, superiority in our markets. The reactions I have noted range from being amusing to tragic. Having led some eight study tours of executives from Textron, Inc. and Avco Corporation to Japan, I have observed that some of my companions downplay everything they saw: "Oh, we have been doing that in the United States for years now. I see nothing new that we can use," to "They really do know their people and give them a degree of participative support that we lack!" Unfortunately, when many returned to their parent company, it was business as usual. They just *didn't have time* to reconstruct their management style to emphasize the fact that people were indeed the foundations for competitive success, but people needed to be inspired and given an opportunity to exercise their talents to identify problems and generate new approaches to continually improve their company's competitive advantage.


## UNDERSTANDING THE COMPETITION

For a number of years, many in U.S. management have underestimated either the potential or the perseverance of the Japanese as industrial competitors. "Yes, they go in there with their Toyota or Honda or Nissan and cut into our sales a bit. But don't worry, we've always had the American buyer in our pocket. He'll come running back when we whistle," they say (spoken in the manner of an elephant indifferently considering a fly on the toenail of its left front foot).

But the American sports car buyer, we have discovered, enjoys the feel and responsiveness of the Nissan 300ZX and the Mazda RX7; American families appreciate the solid, compact lines of the Honda Accord; and the Nissan Pathfinder's living-room-quality stereo and solid, nonrattling body appeal to many American drivers.

Those who wait for the Japanese to fall off the horse through their own clumsiness may wait quite a while. Reacquisition of a solid quality work philosophy in the United States is much more likely to unseat the Japanese.

Korea is also waiting in the wings to come center stage if and when the Japanese price themselves out of the market. The Koreans share the Japanese view that customers deserve quality, and they enjoy the advantage (over Japanese and American producers) of a lower cost of labor.

### Cultural Differences
Citation of cultural differences as the reason for Japan's competitive advantage is too often wishful thinking. While the Japanese lack of resources and space, plus their advantage of a common language and ethnic homogeneity, have been motivating factors, their prime advantage has been in their personal understanding of the value of management knowing and reacting accordingly, *in detail*, to the needs and desires of *both* their internal and external customers. Granted, there are cultural differences between Japan and the United States, but these are not key to Japanese success in my opinion.

Take the preparation and service of food. To eat in a Japanese restaurant in Japan is not just nourishment—it is a memorable experience. The care with which each vegetable and meat or fish entree is prepared is not unlike an artistic performance. There is more attention and care devoted to the production of a sandwich in the deli of a Japanese department store than there is to most sit-down dinners in our better restaurants in the United States. And it is not all showmanship to take your mind off the taste of food. The food tastes as good as it looks. That's quality!

Can we duplicate the degree of commitment to detail? The Marysville, Ohio, experience of Honda; Sony's experience in San Diego; MAZAK's in Florence, Kentucky; and Nissan's in Smyrna, Tennessee, prove there's nothing wrong with the American worker culturally that leadership, guidance, and the establishment of standards won't cure. (Perhaps food preparation and flower arrangement, which the Japanese have a particular knack for, are exceptions. Let's hope the proliferation of American fast-food franchises along the Ginza won't cause one of these unique Japanese talents to become extinct.)

There are, however, examples of American ability to attend to detail in food preparation. Consider Bruce and Kathy Gore, young Americans engaged in quality salmon harvest and preparation in Alaska. In their operation, each fish is hand carried, hand rubbed, and hand glazed—a perfect silvery specimen with not a broken scale and certainly none of the bruises that mar an average salmon—the Rolls Royce of frozen fish.

"When I first fished for salmon, we used pitchforks. Now I massage them; I am like a mortician, trying to make fish look better than they did in life," Bruce Gore told Phyllis C. Richman, *Washington Post* food critic and writer.[1] This is quality—by an American couple who understands, as do the Japanese, that the customer is important and must be catered to and cultivated to keep the customer coming back.

### Japanese Protectionism

"You cannot penetrate the Japanese market. Japan, Inc., is happy to export, but don't try to crack their domestic market. Their protectionist attitude creates a barbed wire fence around that country."

True or false? Either answer will net you partial credit. Japanese quality standards are so high that you will see very few of the Big Three U.S. automakers' products on the road, other than U.S. government vehicles. But the truth of the matter is that, for the most part, the quality of our U.S. products is inadequate to meet Japanese standards. Given the cost of our imports, the Japanese want to be sure before they buy that these goods are *at least* comparable in quality to domestically produced products.

"Yes, their quality is as good as advertised," says Bill Panttaga of Borg-Warner Kabushiki Kaisha. "They like our technology and know-how, but they don't like our inattention to detail. For example, one of our products will have a scratch on the casing and they'll reject it, even though the component is otherwise perfect. They just smile and say, "If you're indifferent to how it looks on the outside, where we can visually inspect it, what will it be like on the inside?"

Al Nakano, president of Kulicke and Soffa (Japan, Ltd.), a stateside company that produces electronic wire-bonding machines, confirms the Japanese view of U.S. indifference to cosmetic appearances and operational defects. His company's machines cost twice as much as their Japanese counterparts, but they are superior, and after some redesign to meet Japanese desires, he has been able to move his product. His counsel to those who would seek Japanese market penetration is that they must try to understand cultural differences, offer a quality product, and exercise extreme patience.

Motorola and Westinghouse (incidentally two of the initial winners of the prestigious MBNQA) as well as Hewlett-Packard and Texas Instruments have demonstrated that the Japanese market can be penetrated—provided U.S. management is willing to put forth both the effort and has the patience to convince the Japanese industrial hierarchy and MITI that they are in for the "long haul."

## THE KING OF THE HILL SYNDROME

Another management belief is that we have a God-given right as Americans to be superior in all things. It's hard to argue that we have not been blessed to an incredible extent by geography and resources. Neither Canada to our north nor Mexico to our south can claim equivalent advantages. Our form of government, capitalistic economy, climate, and free and open society are also unique blessings. But, to feel that these are givens, that we need do nothing to preserve our blessings, is wishful thinking of the grossest sort.

It was the arrival of English and European settlers, with the technology, who came in search of religious and political freedom, that began the development of this nation into an internationally recognized, compassionate, opportunity-offering, and industrially and technologically advanced country. It was the blood, sweat, tears, and efforts of people with an indomitable will to be free and to succeed who accomplished, in a historically short period of time, the modern-day miracle, the United States of America, that stands as a shining example of the efforts and ingenuity of man, God's stellar creation. But preservation and improvement of our assets will require ingenuity and effort.

To be king of the hill is no sin, as long as one recognizes the elements that made that achievement possible. Arrogance, incidentally, is not one of those elements, but arrogance is an attribute that has contributed significantly to the downfall of quality in America.

Art and literature offer examples that help make the point: An artist or writer who becomes famous after years of developing technique and talent often becomes lazy, self-centered, and arrogant because he can peddle anything on the strength of his name and reputation. He can peddle it until he finds himself swept off the hill by fresh talent that is willing to put forth the competitive effort to succeed.

U.S. industry has followed a similar course. Willing to work diligently and with purpose, industry has given this nation the highest standard of living and affluence in the world. World War II, with its ravages of the industrial production system in Europe and the Far East, left the United States the undisputed king of the industrial hill. The three decades that followed created a "thus-it-is-and-thus-it-will-ever-be" self-ordination as far as industrial superiority was concerned. Management then turned its attention to exotic technology and high profits as the twin gods of production, without much thought to either the customer's desires or quality of the product.

Japan flung down the gauntlet and challenged our industrial superiority and our customers' loyalty. It is now essential that we accept the opportunity we have to reestablish ourselves as masters of the indomitable competitive spirit.

## PEOPLE: THE ELEMENT OF SUCCESS

The final misconception is that people play no great role in attaining quality. In this age of high technology, computers, numerical control, computer numerical control, and flexible manufacturing systems, who needs people? Indeed, it is argued that, with the further development of robots and automation, the need for people (an unpredictable and often disagreeable barrier to management's success) may soon be removed. Won't automated factories of the future do away with the need for people? Absolutely not.

Fanuc, located near Mt. Fujiyama and Lake Yamonaka, has robots producing and testing robot components. The factory is large, poorly lighted, and unusually quiet. Robots don't need light to work, and they have no conversation other than the hum of their DC motors. Across the street, robots produce those DC motors. Automated carts make the rounds of each robot machining center to deliver motor components to production and assembly centers.

But, even in this highly roboticized plant, there are human workers. Why? The president and CEO, Dr. S. Inaba, explains: "Every six hours, machines must have chips removed from cutting and grinding tables. I've not yet been able to devise a machine that will accomplish that job on site."

Farther down the line, human workers put on bell housings. Why men instead of machines? Says Inaba, "The fit is most important, and I've not been able to design a machine with the visual-touch sensitivity that man can experience."

Regrettably, the development of automation and mass production lines have desensitized management to the difference between the sensibilities of man vs. the objectivity of machines. We find it easier, at times, to keep our inanimate machinery lubricated than to keep our subordinates stroked. Unlubricated, the former will wear extensively and finally grind to a halt. The latter, unlubricated by recognition, reward, and understanding, will continue to work, but at a slower rate; they'll become indifferent to what they're doing, and the result will manifest itself in poor product and service quality.

Machines can't communicate unhappiness with treatment accorded; nor can they influence the other machines. However, humans can. Unstroked, they become discontented and communicate this, which can have epidemic-like consequences.

Frequent layoffs and forced early retirements have contributed to the scope of U.S. quality problems. F. A. Schaeffer and Dr. C. E. Koop, in their interesting treatment of this question in *Whatever Happened to the Human Race?*, state, "Those who regard individuals as expendable raw materials—to be molded, exploited, then discarded—do battle on many fronts with those who see each person as unique and special, worthwhile, and irreplaceable."[2]

People *are* important. At times they are the most unpredictable resource in one's network of responsibilities, but that should represent a challenge and a potential in the achievement of quality. People require your time and attention, but they are worth it. They create the computers and the programs; they write the symphonies and do the paintings that are timeless in their message and originality. No question about it—people are quality's most important resource.

**Middle Management**
While mobility in any organization is essential for motivation of a junior comer, the rapid mobility of U.S. management is ridiculous. Estimates in 1983 were that top managers normally hold their positions an average of three and one-half years. This means frequent direction and policy changes that break the continuity of purpose, planning, and ongoing programs. Trying to learn the new boss's idiosyncrasies, interests, and management style while simultaneously keeping all the balls in the air can damage productivity. While it can be argued that frequent change brings in fresh ideas, the penalty often is that ideas of the previous regime are discounted before they have had time to mature. Additionally, the new top men may not be in the job long enough to be held accountable for any eggs they may lay.

Mobility in top management can also have a completely disquieting effect on long-range strategic planning. Anxious to see their own ideas play, short-term managers will be interested in establishing short-range productivity and revenue-producing goals that can be readily realized. This approach can be very hard on both personnel and the company over the long term.

One of the most critical responsibilities of management is long-range planning. It permits investment in capital improvements, research and development goals, work satisfaction enhancing programs, expansion plans—the rudiments of sound management. Next to an ignorance about the value of quality in the survival and growth cycle, management has been most delinquent in its long-range planning responsibilities.

**NOTES**

1. Phyllis C. Richman, "Silver Harvest," *Washington Post*, September 17, 1985, sec. D1, p. 16.
2. Francis A. Schaeffer and C. Everett Koop, M.D., *Whatever Happened to the Human Race?* (Old Tappan, N.J.: Flemming H. Revell, 1979), 16.

# 5 QUALITY IN EUROPE

Europe's reputation for quality lasted longer than its real ability to produce that quality because we "provincials in the colonies" revel in ownership of anything made in one of the big three—England, France, and Germany. At one time our assessment was based on recognition of the fact that, prior to automation and production lines, our European ancestors were excellent craftspeople. If you wanted the best watch, you bought one with a Swiss movement. A photographer who could afford the best would buy a German-made Leica. The best china was France's famous Limoges or Haviland, and Irish Waterford crystal was the best crystal to be had. The world-class automobile was Rolls Royce, and the prestigious sports cars were Jaguar and Porsche. Note how many European leaders have been edged out by Oriental contenders.

## IGNORING THE STATE OF THE ART

During a visit to Frankfurt, I listened to Hans-Juran Meyer, vice president and senior manager of the quality department of MAN's Mechanical and Structural Division, one of Germany's largest conglomerates producing a range of items from railroad trains to wind generators. I could close my eyes and imagine I was in the United States listening to a large defense manufacturer brief me on his plant's letter-perfect MIL-Q-9858A system. Meyer knows what is required to achieve quality.

"But does top management participate in MAN's quality program?" I asked during my visit. The engineer shook his head sadly and said, "I have little success in getting them involved."

This is another example of management's being self-satisfied and ignoring the competition. In my several trips to Europe, I have never come upon any dearth of knowledge about what *needs* to be done, but there is a definite gap between that and what *is* being done.

## PERCEIVED PROBLEM AREAS

Perhaps the greatest contributor to Europe's quality problem is ignorance. While Europe's industry suffered much the same destruction as Japan's during World War II, the Europeans had a well-established quality reputation prior to that. They had merely to pick up where they left off after the war. Why didn't that happen?

At least two major disturbances occurred: one cultural, one technological.

Culturally, U.S. affluence and our postwar occupation of Europe affected European culture in much the same manner that we affected Japan and Korea. America's informality, and lack of respect for age and position, and a relaxed work ethic—all of these—while ignored by the older generation, were quickly accepted by European young people, producing a subculture that rebelled against established lines of discipline and authority.

Albert Schunck, foreign liaison director for I.G. Metalle, Germany's largest union, described the change that took place in Germany's work force. He mentions an increase in absenteeism and a growing indifference to both the work ethic and dedication to perfection once commonplace in the Teutonic culture. And, he says, "With the exception of Volkswagen, industry has not really given robotics much thought." Herein lies the second impact—technology.

The 1970s, 1980s, and 1990s, building on the technology ushered in by both the nuclear and space ages, have seen the evolution of electronic and mechanical complexity in industry, quantum in nature and scope. Tolerances are much less forgiving than before, requiring more diligence and know-how. I suggest that the decreased concern of the work force, coupled with the increased technological requirement, caused Europe's quality problem.

### Documentation of the "Hidden Factory"

Europeans have yet to pay much attention to costs. This is perhaps the most important step that European industry can take to avoid the hazards the United States has experienced and is still experiencing. Until one knows what and how much those hidden factory costs are, one cannot begin to solve the problems caused by nonconformance: poor quality, high scrap, and high rework.

I'll venture a studied guesstimate that Europe will meet its quality Waterloo in three to five years if European management doesn't awaken to a few of the facts of life such as specified in ISO 9000 regarding the essence of quality and how it is achieved. Hand wringing and exhortation won't solve the problem. Evaluation and action will.

## INTERNATIONAL VENDOR FLAVOR

Europe is unique in that it's a community of sovereign nations, occupying a limited geographic area. This gives rise to marketing agreements that include co-production and multinational vendor coordination. This may be the most treacherous collection of tightropes any quality manager has to walk. Imagine yourself having to monitor and require quality of a vendor with whom you have a significant marketing potential. The danger of cross-cultural clashes demands diplomatic and politic negotiators.

### International Market Orientation

In the United States, there is not a paucity of domestic market; in Europe, almost every industry has a foreign market just outside its very limited geographical borders. This may contribute to Europeans' apparent indifference to foreign competition. They have never known anything *but* foreign competition. However, the continental competition they have experienced is acceptably softened by a polite live-and-let-live understanding. The competition from the Far East plays hardball, and, while tariff barriers and quotas may stave them off initially, public demand will require that such artificial barriers eventually be lifted or competitive quality be achieved. The Common Market coalition into a United States of Europe-like structure will have some impact, quite possibly making stiffer the competition we have to face from Europe. That remains to be determined. Issuance of ISO 9000 as the standard for doing business with European firms is a given that must be considered by U.S. firms. While I believe that the 20 areas listed in the ISO 9001 Quality System Model published by British Standards Institute (BSi) are implicit in MIL-Q-9858A, the ISO does well to spell it out since people appear to need more specificity in how to set up an effective quality system. The essentials of ISO 9000 are contained in Appendix G.

## POSITIVE ASPECTS OF AND SUCCESSFUL
## COMPANIES IN EUROPEAN INDUSTRY

There are a number of European management approaches that might bear emulating. One involves relationships with unions. I. G. Metalle's Albert Schunck explains the co-determination relationship German unions enjoy with management: Two levels of involvement exist, with one union level at the company supervisory level and the second tier at the management-director level. Numerically, the supervisory-level union leaders equal plant-level members. At the management-director level, there are fewer union members and they have perhaps less influence, but they exercise what Schunck terms a co-determination influence on issues such as "rules of the house," daily work hours, bonuses, holiday planning, and company social schemes. He points out that this is important since, under German law, the government can't intervene in strikes as the U.S. government can. Management's willingness to allow unions a voice in policy matters, even though not of parity status with management, apparently has contributed much to union/management harmony.

Unions are concerned about Japanese competition, but quality is not recognized as the issue. "Lower prices through higher production is the key," says Schunck. The inescapable relationship of quality and productivity is not yet appreciated, or so it would appear.

### Quality Circles

By and large, European industry considered quality circles a Japanese cultural phenomenon that had little value in Europe. The Citroen assembly plant in Rennes, France, was an exception. At Citroen, assembly workers were enthusiastic about their quality circles, and they reported that management was seriously interested in their input. The 11 circle members I interviewed in one circle claimed their circle provided an active channel of communication with their bosses regarding production procedures, working conditions, and personnel problems. The circle members' responses demonstrated a great depth of understanding.

A. Genovese, plant manager, and L. Mercier, quality manager, obviously established quality circles on a solid foundation. According to Rene Le Gall, quality engineer for Citroen, the Rennes facility is Citroen's quality pacesetter.

### Extensive Test Programs

Opel's assembly plant southwest of Frankfurt is an example of what extensive training does for quality. While rejecting quality circles, this plant achieves quality by subjecting its components, from seat fabrics to shock absorbers, to extreme life-cycle dynamic testing. They do no source inspection, but they perform 100 percent receiving inspections. And, Opel was looking at robotics in the paint shop and in some areas of welding as essential to maintaining competitive status.

One feature that makes the Opel a popular car in Europe is the integration of service into the producer's quality system. This provides comprehensive feedback for design and material corrective action.

## Documentation
Telefonbau and Normalzeit, Germany's leader in both communications and alarm systems, demonstrated an excellent data-gathering and evaluation system. An automated system for data storage permits the company to retrieve data and determine trends. This ensures correction of problems before they become customer-related.

## Apprentice Training
One of the long-standing strengths of German industry is apprentice training. At Zettlemeyer, a subsidiary of IBH located in Konz, 8 percent of the work force is in an apprentice program. It includes an exceptionally well-equipped classroom and shop area where apprentices spend half of their day under instruction. They spend the remainder on the production floor under the supervision of an expert in the craft being learned. This three-year program ensures a continuity of talent and contributes significantly to Zettlemeyer's quality.

Heinrich Von Prittwitz, managing director of sales and service for Zettlemeyer, explained on my visit there that, while the firm was slow in embracing robotics, 60 percent of its machinery was numerically controlled or computer numerically controlled. Between 1981 and 1982, Zettlemeyer reduced scrap from 2.5 percent to 1.8 percent and was continuing on a downtrend.

## Quality Systems
SNECMA, one of France's larger producers of aircraft engines and landing gear, has a comprehensive quality system.

MATRA, a giant conglomerate with 11 major product lines, ranging from missiles to automobiles, represents a company on the leading edge of technology. Its extremely sophisticated test and evaluation facility is impressive; not so its lack of scrap and rework documentation.

**Unique Approach to DeFODing**
Dassault's plant at Argenteuil, a suburb of Paris, assembles the fuselage of the Mirage 2000 and F-1 jet fighters. There were two significant innovations in this plant. The first one is that all new production models are first assembled by quality personnel. This gives the QA people first-hand knowledge of the problems that production assemblies may create, and, of even greater benefit, provides instant feedback to Dassault's major design/prototype facility in St. Cloud via a computer-aided design/manufacturing (CADM) system. This marriage of production, quality, and design ensures quality products on delivery.

Foreign-object damage (FOD) has been a significant cause of rework in U.S. overhaul and rework contractors' plants. Dassault's J. Y. Lazard explained that his firm solved the problem by rotating the jig-mounted fuselage around its horizontal axis. Everything not secure drops out. This second innovation is both practical and ingenious. *Vive la France.*

**Renault—Coming up Fast**
During my visit to Renault's plant in Flins in 1982 I learned they produce 22 percent of Renault's worldwide output of 8000 autos per day. Flins wasn't at that time Renault's most automated plant, but the fully automated corrosion control plant was impressive. It took all the guesswork and opportunity for human error out of this important process. Welding was largely automated, and electrodes are replaced before they reach 50 percent of advertised life. This produced welds that were less than 0.03 percent defective. Unlike Toyota, where anyone is not only authorized but *encouraged* to stop the production line when a defect is detected, at Flins, no one short of the upper management level was authorized to stop the 1800-car-per-day line. "We just hope the customer doesn't find the defect," said a spokesperson, who understandably did not wish to be identified. This situation reflects a tendency of too many U.S. industries where production is the key and quality is supported only to the extent that it does not hinder the production quota.

**Quality in Composites**
Since 1970, Dassault's composite fabrication and test facility in Biarritz on the southwestern coast of France has used composites for control, high-stress, and access panels on the Mirage III, F-1, Mirage 4000, 2000, Alfa jet, and Falcon 50, the last of which is being purchased by the U.S. Coast Guard. Dassault began development of its composite capability in the Jaguar, but the first flight test of a composite in aircraft was in the Mirage II in 1975. Documentation of composite process control at Dassault is comprehensive.

Dassault works closely with Surveillance Industrielle De L'Armement (SIAR), the French Ministry of Defense counterpart to the quality section of the U.S. Defense Logistics Agency. Complete composite lamination is developed by the local design department of Dassault Biarritz, then approved by both SIAR and corporate quality before going into production. This assured a sound review process. All changes go the same route. Dassault is essentially establishing composite quality standards in France. In fact, some U.S. aircraft and space giants looked to Dassault for ideas in this technological breakthrough.

Vendor control is achieved by specifying process control procedures, auditing compliance, and then double-checking by receiving inspection.

Environmental control is most critical. Temperatures must be kept between 20°C and 70°C, and relative humidity between 40 and 70 percent. These same standards apply to stowage of the carbon, fibers, and resins. Since there are no French sources for fibers, these are imported from the United States, United Kingdom, and Japan.

Application and curing are delicate processes, and Dassault's evaluation of the effectiveness of the composite's bonding is accomplished by both X-ray and ultrasonic inspection. Results are printed out in color-coded graphics. Dassault claims to produce less than 1 percent scrap. They did not offer specifics about rework.

Dassault's assembly plant in Merignac offers an example of the contribution a stout work ethic can make to quality. Assembly line organization and cleanliness reflect the pride in workmanship these aircraft assemblers have in the fruits of their labor.

## PRESENT VS. FUTURE

By using examples of French and German industries that I visited, I've attempted to paint a work picture of quality in Europe. As a member of the NATO quality group that planned the 1984 symposium in Paris, I'm fairly convinced that these two countries are representative of quality in the United Kingdom, Italy, and Belgium. From this, I believe a number of observations can be drawn.

First, why have some major European industries succeeded while the United States has taken severe, damaging hits? The relationship between management and unions (the concept of co-determination), the recognition that layoffs damage continuity of skill and morale of craftspeople, that slowdowns are preferable, and that, as management goes, so goes the worker—all of these have combined to make European industry more sensitive to the need for a team approach to manufacturing. Recent events indicate this may be catching on in the United States.

European automobile and aircraft industries tend to better identify poor design early on rather than delegating the function to the customer. As was implied by Alfred Schunck, Japanese industry still leads in this area.

The teaming of apprentice with expert in a formal, tiered training program ensures knowledgeable craftspeople.

Finally, the basic European work ethic contributes significantly to quality in Europe.

The four factors summarized—union-management relationships, more stringent test scenarios, apprentice training programs, and work ethic—comprise the basic underpinnings of quality in Europe.

## But, on the Other Hand . . .

While there were a number of positive areas in which European industry may take pride, there were warning signs that they may be approaching the same hazardous section of road on Competition Parkway that the United States has been navigating with great pain for several years. One of the warning signs is the lack of preoccupation by European management and customers alike with quality. This is a condition almost guaranteed to induce a quality crisis. While Japanese quality is recognized, there appears to be little concern over what this can mean to the European economy and industrial competitiveness.

While European workers and consumers aren't yet as affluent as their U.S. counterparts, they are not far behind. Such affluence can have a serious impact on worker motivation and job satisfaction. Failure to appreciate the value of robotics and automation to the extent the Japanese have will have a serious effect on Europe's competitive marketing of a quality product. While the very affluent can afford the exclusive hand tooling of a Rolls Royce, the average person who would like to have a car comparable in styling and reliability cannot. That person must rely on industry to bring cost down and reliability up. This can be most reasonably accomplished by automation and use of robotics.

The indifference to quality circles can also work to European industry's disservice. Europe's ethnic homogeneity gives its quality circles great promise and a solid potential for identifying and solving problems before they get out of hand.

Quality control in Europe, regrettably, is still based primarily on final inspection. As discussed previously, with low-volume and relatively simple products, this approach may be considered acceptable in some circles. However, when high volume and complex products are involved, process control is the only way to assure quality.

# 6 SIXTY RUNGS IN JAPAN'S QUALITY LADDER

"He who wrestles with us strengthens our nerves and sharpens our skills. Our antagonist is our helper."

Edmund Burke

If success is an excuse for deification, we have transformed Japan into a place of worship, and the pilgrimages of our business community to Japan were probably justified. Without question, in the past several years, many books and articles have been written on Japanese industrial success. Books by Japanese and American authors quickly reach best-seller status, confirming the fact that U.S. businessmen and customers alike are mesmerized by this rags-to-riches phenomenon in which the United States played a major role.

Is this an academic exercise Americans are going through, similar to our armchair reaction to television's bad news from around the world? Is this a self-flagellation to atone for the years we slept in self-satisfied stupor, confident no one could approach us industrially? Let's hope there's more to the widespread interest in our worthy competitors.

And let's do more than scratch the surface of the phenomena that transformed "Made in Japan" from a label signifying *cheap* to one signifying quality, reliability, and preference.

The Japanese quality phenomenon is not the product of just quality circles, top management involvement, MITI protectionism, better education, or more disciplined workers. It is the product of 60 or more different factors, all of which affect the issue of quality to a significant degree.

First of all, their success has been a direct result of market research and a focus on quality. During my visit to Komatsu headquarters, Osamu Takahashi,

63

managing director and general manager of Komatsu's R&D division, described it. "In 1961, Caterpillar's capture of the Japanese tractor market made us realize we had to do something drastic to stay in business. We concluded that quality offered the biggest payoff. Our chairman announced a QC campaign in 1962. In 1963, we instituted quality circles, and in 1964, we won the coveted Deming Prize for quality. We built on the momentum that recognition gave us and, in 1981, we won Japan's highest honor for quality, The Japan Quality Control Award. We attribute these achievements to two things: research to determine market needs and preferences, and *quality*— fulfilling expectations the customer had specified or those we had created during marketing."

The late Kaoru Ishikawa, former president of Musashi Institute of Technology (MIT), was equally frank during my initial visit to MIT. "After the years of deprivation caused by World War II, Japan began producing goods for the consumer market. Initially, we were sacrificing quality for production, and we earned a reputation for producing cheap junk. With the help of Deming and Juran, we began educating management to the need for quality. It was a top-down effort that eventually concentrated on first-line supervisors, since we felt they could communicate best with workers in the plants. This campaign included seminars, public radio broadcasts, quality control circles, and publication of *Gemba to QC* (a magazine, *QC for Foremen*) in 1962. This monthly compilation of quality circle information was renamed FQC in 1973. It is an extremely well-read journal.

When asked whether he thought quality circles are viable in Western societies, Ishikawa replied, "Yes. Though the Buddhist mentality more easily lends itself to QC, I believe circles can profitably be used with some modifications in any culture." He cited Singapore, where three vastly differing cultures (Islamic-Malays; Buddhist-Chinese; Hindu-Indian/South Pacific) are mixed in an industrial society whose annual per capita productivity rivals that of Japan.

Considering the interest displayed by the former Soviet Union in the past five years regarding the issue of quality and how to achieve it, it makes sense that the new Confederation of Independent States (CIS), in its bid to enter the world marketplace, will be interested in the concept of quality control circles. Without them, entry will be most difficult.

The following factors are not prioritized in any manner. They are simply 60 factors that, in my opinion, have contributed to Japan's dramatic postwar industrial recovery and its challenge to the world's other leading producer nations.

*1. Lifetime employment.*   By and large, Japanese workers retire at 60, though the government encourages workers to stay till 65. Once accepted for employment (especially in larger companies), they are *guaranteed* employment with that company. And, according to Masaharu Odaki, deputy general manager of Keihin works of Nippon Kokan Steel Company (NKK), "Very few workers leave the firm after their second or third year." Tenure doesn't demotivate workers, Odaki says, "because workers recognize that their semi-annual bonuses depend on the economic vitality of the firm." At Komatsu, these often total about 10 extra months of pay per year. In addition, perks include housing for unmarrieds, home loans for newlyweds, promise and fact of upward mobility within the company, access to an employee cafeteria, uniforms, and partially subsidized holiday trips.

Teruhisa Tanaka, manager of technological coordination (with NKK for 20 years), says he wouldn't consider leaving the firm even if he could get a substantially better position and salary. "Absolutely not. I will remain here till I retire," he says. "I am NKK and NKK is me."

Lifetime employment gives Japanese industry the advantage of a stable, experienced work force. The United States, on the other hand, is a mobile and ambition-driven society. Lifetime employment here is primarily practiced by very large industries. Where practiced, it is a definite factor in quality.

*2. Company unions.*   This approach to unionization lends itself to a better understanding between management and worker. Noriyuki Sugihara, ex-president of the company union at Yokogowa Hewlett-Packard (YHP), cites an example of the difference between Japanese and American unions. Asked whether he thinks his one-time constituents deserved a bigger piece of the profit pie, he replies, "No. My feeling is that quality improves productivity and, as productivity grows and we become more competitive, the 'pie' grows. We don't look for a bigger piece of the pie, just a larger pie."

*3. Bonus plans.*   Most Japanese companies pay bonuses twice a year. These aren't bonuses in the strictest definition, but *saved pay*—an enforced saving that enables workers to make major purchases such as appliances or automobiles, to invest in postal savings, or to make a down payment on a house. In essence, it is a fiscal-year cushion to both company and employee. As noted earlier, it can amount to almost a year's pay. It is a negotiated bonus in which union and management leaders participate (separate from pay negotiations).

The bonus system provides management flexibility to deal with market surges or recessions, since bonuses are conditional on meeting productivity targets. Should the market sour, should sales or profits fall, the company can reduce or withhold bonuses. Not a pleasant prospect, but workers prefer the loss of a bonus to being laid off during slow times.

Many workers invest their bonuses in Japan's famous *postal savings*. These provide modest interest rates to the investor and serve as a source of expansion capital for industry. This keeps industry from having to depend on a reduced money market, with its high interest rates caused primarily by increased government borrowing.

*4. Ethnic homogeneity of work force.*    This has obvious advantages and obvious disadvantages. Japan controls its immigration and thus maintains a cultural homogeneity of its work force. Management and labor share a language and cultural background, and goal regimentation of the Japanese work force is therefore much easier than in our heterogeneous society.

Our many languages and cultural backgrounds in the United States—as well as our emphasis on freedom of thought and the individual—encourage questions, opposition, and disagreement. Our system has given birth to some of the greatest technological advances and has precluded ambitious rulers from leading us into national self-destruction by exploiting a national chauvinism, but a homogeneous society like Japan's is more adaptable to concepts like quality control circles and participatory management. When everyone's thought process is similar, it is easy to recruit a Kamikazi pilot. However, independent and diverse thinking can do wonders in the development of technology and the introduction of innovation. While the Japanese think "we," Americans think "I."

*5. Top management involvement in quality.*    Japan's executives are personally involved with both the details and personnel of their business. Managers know their personnel and can greet them by name because managers get out on the shop floor, meet them, observe what they are doing, and converse about problems. Management knows the details of their company's quality strategy since they are directly involved in its derivation and implementation.

Executives of all the Japanese firms I've ever visited wear the same uniforms as their workers, so it is difficult to identify them as top management. Their presentations, which key in on what they are doing to promote quality, quickly reinforce their understanding, and, best of all, their involvement in quality. The total quality control system and top management QC audit are two examples of top management involvement.

6. *Quality control circles.*    Quality control circles are a way of life in Japanese industry. The Union of Japanese Scientists and Engineers (JUSE) estimates that since circles were introduced in Japan in 1960, the movement has grown to include more than a million circles with up to 14 million members, although only 350,047 circles with 2,702,289 members are registered with JUSE. As mentioned before, the monthly *FQC* published by JUSE provides a vehicle to share quality and productivity suggestions and achievements throughout all industry. It appears to be widely read and is keyed to workers and first-line supervisors.

Since 1971, JUSE has sponsored competitions to recognize those circles that produce the most innovative and valuable quality improvement suggestions. Circles normally meet on company time, either weekly, biweekly, or monthly. At Nissan, in Oppama, circles meet during lunch, during breaks, or after work. That demonstrates the ultimate motivation.

Masumasa Imaizumi, of the quality and standards department at Nippon Kokan Steel, lists 10 characteristics of circles: self-development, voluntary participation, group activity, participation by all, application of QC techniques, activities relevant to the place of work, enlivening motivation for longevity's sake, mutual enlightenment, creativity and innovation, and consciousness of and thirst for quality improvement.

Sueo Ohnaka, manager of the special electronics engineering department of Fujitsu, said the firm has 2600 quality circles. All suggestions generated by the circles are evaluated and the best are sent to top management. There are bonuses for the best ideas.

It is easy to see that circles not only solve problems but also broaden the workers' outlook, education, social intercourse, interpersonal relationships, growth, and understanding that anything that profits their company profits them.

7. *Use of robotics and automation.*    Despite what American standards would represent as 4 percent unemployment, Japanese industry claims a shortage in skilled labor. (They quote unemployment at 2 percent.) To augment the human work force, Japanese industrialists have embraced automation and robotics. The United States may hold a slight edge in the development of robots, but, in 1982, 59 percent of the world's robotics *applications* were found in Japanese industry. A prolific use is in the Oppama plant of Nissan, where robotic welding arms quickly and quietly slither through auto frame lightening holes to tack weld, retract, and head for another hole. These arms resemble eels playing hide and seek in a labyrinth.

Sadao Fujii, manager of Fujitsu's production technology development section, displayed robots being developed by the company. When asked about possible resentment by workers at being displaced by robots, he stated, "We concentrate on developing robots to do menial, repetitive, dirty, or dangerous jobs that workers do not like. Also, you must understand that we have a skilled labor shortage in Japan, and robots allow us to release workers to be retrained and take other positions." Fujii does admit that, at some time in the future, robots may compete with humans for more desirable jobs.

Robotics contribute significantly to productivity and quality. Cost of installation is quickly amortized by replacement of increasingly expensive human workers, the elimination of rework, the reduction of lighting and air conditioning requirements, and by reprogrammability. Most industries appear to be developing and programming their own robots, buying off-the-shelf components and designing systems to fill corporate needs.

8. *Economic challenge.*   Quality consciousness was Japan's basic answer to the economic challenge the country faced after World War II, when the reputation of Japanese consumer goods as cheap junk was associated with this manufacturing-oriented nation. Nippon Steel spoke of its inability to produce quality steel rapidly enough to be competitive. This led the firm to adopt automation.

An interesting sidelight was Nippon's claim that the environmental protection standards at their Kawasaki plant were stiffer than those found in the U.S. steel industry. (Twenty percent of NKK's initial $5 billion capital investment was spent to install pollution controls; 10 percent of annual operating costs keeps the systems operative.)

Nippon Steel uses no oil for its energy needs; 93 percent of its energy is provided by coal or coke, the rest by gas. They say they have become the fifth largest world steel producer (second largest in Japan) because of modern facilities, people, and technology. They boasted of 1320 quality circles encompassing 8500 workers, and scrap and rework at a level of 7 percent compared to 27 percent in the U.S. steel industry during my visits.

9. *Cultural proclivity for attention to detail.*   Japanese gardens are living poetry, with neatly trimmed grass, flowers, and trees. Japanese restaurants have an equal concern for taste, appearance, and gracious service. The island is a "nation of inches" in the words of Ed Graham, in which every space, movement, and creation is optimized to ensure harmony with surroundings, usability, and appeal to the greatest numbers. This attitude carries over into industry.

*10. Superior education system.*    Japan enjoys a 99 percent literacy rate—better than that of most nations documenting such achievement. Primary and secondary schools work students hard and produce those who compete strenuously to gain admittance to prestigious colleges. The Japanese embassy points out that these students relax somewhat in college, but their commitment to secondary education lays the groundwork for a work force that understands effort as the key to success. Secondary education also prepares workers who, because of their literacy, understand procedures and instructions better than Americans. Japanese schools concentrate on producing engineers rather than lawyers and accountants.

*11. Commitment to training.*    The Japanese don't believe workers can learn to produce quality by accumulating hands-on hours as do many American contractors. Formal training is a way of life, and Japanese industry provides resources to this vital area to ensure that workers know what they are doing. The concept that a lifetime employee is a part of the company's assets is reiterated time and again. As a company invests more and more in training, employees more and more become living assets, to be shifted to greater responsibilities and new positions. Japan's low unemployment rate (in a work environment with the highest application of robotics) demonstrates that training and education pay dividends.

Training commitment includes continual development of top executives in settings commensurate with position. JUSE conducts management training seminars at the nation's most plush resorts.

The next level of emphasis is the first-line supervisor—the interface between management and worker. The supervisor's prestige is fortified by discrete training in quality, interpersonal communication, new processes, and trips abroad to observe other nations' productivity efforts. This appears to be accomplished more easily in Japan than in the United States. First-line supervisors are not the unionists. Recall that employees elect company union representatives to convey their desires to management. One of the big advantages of such a company union is that these supervisors are spared union stress—they're just as eligible as anyone else to be elected representatives. They participate in the election of their representative and, then, can turn attention to the task at hand. Likewise, they can concentrate on training as appropriate.

Fujitsu's Institute of Management Training is a classic example of Japanese industry's dedication to training. It includes a mandatory three-month course for executives who reach their 45th birthday. It serves to pump up and reignite these people to preclude any midlife slump.

*12. National unity of effort.*     Industry goals are coordinated by the Japanese Ministry of International Trade and Industry (MITI). Promising industrial ventures are backed by substantial low-interest, long-term loans provided by banking consortiums, MITI plays the role of overseer in negotiating these loans. Short-term return on investment (ROI) is not their goal. Stockholders, though, do become impatient for (ROI), and considerable public relations work is required to convince investors that patience begets growth and profit.

Japanese trading companies (the counterpart of which our nation desperately needs to stimulate trade with developing nations rich in resources but cash poor) play a vital role in arranging barter transactions and local co-production facilities that take advantage of lower labor rates in developing countries.

*13. Supervisor-centered QC training.*     While Juran and Deming were responsible for top-down training and the concept of statistical QC, the Japanese themselves recognized that workers relate much better to first-line supervisors with whom they have constant close contact and to whom they are responsible than they do to top management. Therefore, why not provide first-level supervisors the training and resources to inculcate quality into the worker? They did this in 1962, and the effort has proved remarkably successful.

*14. Financial incentive to the innovative.*     While a pat on the back, a certificate, or an article in the plant paper might be adequate reward for some, Japanese management recognizes that the "yen talks." Those who make special efforts to improve quality and productivity—whether individuals or members of a quality circle—are financially rewarded. The twice-annual bonus is another incentive for increased effort and productivity.

*15. Modern industrial base.*     The Japanese have the United States to thank for this significant edge. After doing a relatively comprehensive job of destroying Japanese industry during World War II, our morality and generosity (plus our national security interest in making Japan self-sufficient) encouraged us to assist Japan financially and technically in rebuilding a modern industrial base. The Japanese are grateful for our help, but this does not deter them from trying to best us in the marketplace.

The war left the United States untouched, so much of our industry still operates with equipment and facilities from before then. We are still recycling 1950 technology in the Industrial Plant Equipment program administered by the DLA.

16. *Quality recognition status.*   A company that believes that it has achieved the high standards of quality required by the 10 JUSE criteria may declare for the Deming Prize and invite the Deming Prize committee to evaluate its organization. The evaluators, all professionals, assess the achievements. The company must convince the committee that it excels in at least seven of the 10 categories. Very few achieve excellence in eight or more.

The 10 criteria are:

- Quality policy of the firm
- Organization and management
- Training and dissemination of quality policy
- Information collection, transmittal, and application
- Analysis—statistical quality control
- Standardization of quality control throughout the organization
- Effectiveness (measure of effectiveness and conformance of pre-estimated result to actual result)
- Quality assurance (safety and preclusion of product liability, process control, preventive maintenance, quality appraisal, and auditing system for assuring quality)
- Effectiveness of quality control
- Future plans to assure continuation of achieved level of product assurance

The evaluated organization must score at least 70 points out of a possible 100 in the above categories to be awarded the Deming recognition. The highest grade the current executive director recalls was in the low 80s.

Five years after winning a Deming Prize, the firm is again examined to see if it has improved in its quality assurance. If it has, the organization is awarded the coveted Japan Quality Control Prize.

The Deming and Japan QC prizes are definite stimuli to quality consciousness in Japanese industry. Factories vie for such recognition, for it has sales value in the Japanese marketplace. Indicative of this was Sumitomo Metal's half-page ad in the August 24, 1981, *Wall Street Journal*, which included a large replica of the Deming medal given for the prize and the headline, "The Greatest Name in Japanese Quality Control Is American." Though they won the award in 1953, Sumitomo still trades on that achievement.

Junji Noguchi, executive director of JUSE, points out that, including the 1992 winners, 55 individuals have won the coveted Deming Medalist Award, and for Deming Application Prize 93 large companies, 34 medium and small enterprises, 5 divisions of 5 companies in the division category, and 15 factories of 14 companies in the factory category have been awarded the Quality Control Award.

The Malcolm Baldrige National Quality Award is the U.S. counterpart to the Deming Prize. The idea for the Baldrige Award was conceived and developed by a small group of interested individuals, including the author; Dr. Jack Grayson, CEO of the American Productivity and Quality Center; LCDR E. M. Graham; Ms. Marty Russell; and a number of others from industry, DOD, ASQC, and NASA. A brief summary of this development appears in Appendix H.

*17. Union of Japanese Scientists and Engineers (JUSE).* This very active organization was established in Japan in 1946 with the specific charter to improve quality. Totally private, as of 1992 it boasted a membership of 1945 companies. Membership is limited to top management.

JUSE's thrust is *training.* As mentioned previously, it publishes the periodical *FQC* and various literature on quality. It sponsors the Deming and Japanese quality competitions, the Ishikawa Award (for individuals making a literary contribution to quality), and an annual quality circle competition. JUSE is an aggressive and potent factor in Japanese quality. There is no connection between JUSE and the Japanese government. Unfortunately, there is presently no U.S. organization with the same ability to broker international attitude, image, and performance of members.

*18. Lack of government intrusion into quality.* What kind of resourcing and control can one get from the Japanese government regarding quality? None. And that's the way Japan's private sector wants it. Comments one hears: "Too much red tape." "Interference and delay." Japan Productivity Center Director Mikio Aoki says, "We find no advantage from government intervention in quality with the possible exception of the coordinating support from MITI in promoting international trade." (Few American politicians or businessmen will agree that that's government's sole role.)

Japan's military production is minuscule by comparison to consumer goods. The Ministry of Defense does monitor the quality performance of defense-related commodities in much the same way our DCAS does, but Japan's defense budget is so small that the consequence of this monitoring is insignificant. (It is interesting to note that MIL-Q-9858A is the model for Japanese conformance standards.)

*19. Administrative reform of government regulations.* Japan's prime minister's Ad Hoc Committee on Regulation Reform focuses on voiding or modifying those regulations deemed liable to hamper industrial growth and quality. All in industry agree that the committee performs a positive function. Committee membership includes nongovernment agencies, such as JUSE and the Japan Productivity Center, as volunteer participants. These overseers ensure minimum government intrusion into the affairs of commerce.

*20. Meticulous analysis of productivity factors and trends.* The Japan Productivity Center was established in 1955, inspired by the Anglo-American Council on Productivity (the model for the European Marshall Recovery Plan). The center was the brainchild of Kohe Goshi, who had traveled to Europe and observed the utility of the Anglo-American Productivity Conference and the European Productivity Agency. Japan Productivity Center Executive Director Aoki points out that, "In Japan, personnel expenditures are considered a fixed cost, much the same as facilities."

Aoki feels that we in America expect too little from workers who, therefore, never realize their full potential. His productivity charts show that, while overall economic productivity in the United States is higher than in Japan, our trend is nearly flat, while Japan still shows a steep upturn. He is certain this indicates that Japan will soon surpass U.S. productivity.

*21. Consensus management.* Japanese managers, unlike their U.S. counterparts, do not make unilateral decisions affecting production, improvements, or quality. An idea or concept is aired for comment by workers and middle management, and these observations and suggestions are all seriously considered by top management. This, of course, prolongs the Japanese decision-making process, but it distributes ownership to the corporate body through involvement and consent. (It also allows *all* to share blame for bad decisions.)

Because top management subscribes to quality control, and because responsibility for decisions is widely distributed, quality is not the compartmentalized concern it sometimes is in U.S. firms. Does this consensus approach preclude top management having the final say? Not at all. What it does is dispel the feeling of arbitrary autonomy.

The Japanese are not comfortable with the top executive making all the decisions. That person is also somewhat uncomfortable in such a role. The principal reason for this is not generally understood by Americans. It is that, if many participants are allowed to comment on an idea or policy change *before* it is locked in concrete, there will be much less resistance to it when implemented. All will identify with the policy and have a feeling of ownership. In addition, consensus affords an immediate review at the action level, which often prevents management from issuing an infeasible mandate. In America, too often we issue the mandate and then spend the next two years trying to have it accepted.

*22. Work ethic.*   Despite American influence on the Japanese customers' tastes in clothes, music, food (I saw more McDonalds, Wendys, and Pizza Huts on the Ginza than might be thought possible), Japanese workers have the same work ethic that the United States had before our workers came to feel they owe little to their companies. The Japanese have been accused of being a nation of workaholics. The statement can be interpreted as demeaning, but they regard it as a compliment.

*23. Resource limitation.*   Japan, with its limited space and paucity of resources, must make the most of all it has. Japan entered World War II seeking territorial and raw material gains. When its military solution failed, it turned to maximizing what it had. Space is at such a premium that it must be exploited with great care and diligence. This colors the Japanese workers' efforts to excel with what little they have—an example of adversity's positive influence.

*24. Early retirement.*   Do Japanese workers enjoy a predictable monthly income from their firms after retirement? In the majority of cases, no. They receive a lump-sum payoff that, together with meager social security benefits, must support them for the rest of their lives after age 60 or 65. As a consequence, they save and invest their bonuses and establish post-retirement "mom-and-pop" businesses, or become suppliers as I'll describe in rung 26. There is an incredible number of small shops and groceries competing for the market.

Supermarkets, for the most part, have not caught on in Japan as they have in the United States. Early retirement keeps the labor market dynamic and does not appear to have been deleterious to individual longevity. Japanese men have the longest life expectancy of any culture—89 years. Of interest is the fact that Nippon Kokan Steel has raised the retirement age of its workers to 60, perhaps bellwethering the rest of Japanese industry, to help employees and the company.

*25. Uninhibited transition from government service to private industry.* Unhampered by the military/industrial complex phobia of the United States, top leaders in industry and commerce frequently are government or military retirees. Instead of starting in business and moving to government after success, the Japanese government bureaucrat, having learned the government organization well, moves to industry and uses his or her knowledge and contacts to promote the economy. It appears to work better than our reverse system.

*26. Hub/spoke development of suppliers.* Japanese industry enjoys high vendor quality because many suppliers are former employees who, having learned the parent companies' systems of quality, set up small bike shops.Understanding quality manufacturing, they can provide quality components with little source inspection and few rejects. Many industries help finance such starts with venture capital. Toyota, for example, has grown 90 percent of its suppliers (according to Japanese embassy estimates) with such venture capital. Competition is keen, and nonconforming producers die, but the surviving organizations are indeed producers.

*27. Application of Juran and Deming principles of quality control.* The Japanese are good listeners, and they are superb adapters of technology. They have no reluctance to exploit others' developments, and they identify with their philosophical and technical quality godfathers: J. M. Juran and W. Edwards Deming. While U.S. and European industry gave scant heed to these quality giants, Japan treated them with respect approaching traditional ancestral worship. The logo of the Deming Prize on a product, such as a Pentel pen, carries as much weight as appointment by Her Majesty, Queen Elizabeth II, does for the selected companies in England.

*28. Market research.* As a Komatsu executive pointed out, their rise to eminence in the heavy construction equipment field was the product of two thrusts—quality and market research—determining what consumers want and giving it to them.

U.S. auto manufacturers failed to perceive that the 1972 fuel crisis would have a real impact on the American buyer and continued to produce large, fuel-inefficient cars. The Japanese, already in small car ascendency, saw a need and filled it. It is interesting to note that several years ago GM conceded this market to the Japanese, stating that they could not produce this type of car as economically as could Japan. More recently, with investment in Saturn, GM threw down the gauntlet and declared itself a competitor for the market. Fortunately for GM, the Saturn is selling well in the United States.

*29. Long-term management outlook.*   Turnover of U.S. top management occurs every three to three-and-a-half years and therefore operates for short-term gains. The Japanese feel that the future is long term. Their investments (hard and soft) aim for growth over the long period. It's not hard to make a tortoise-and-hare analogy: the tortoise with its persistant progress in contest with the hare with its sporadic leaps and bounds.

*30. Industry commitment to research.*   The Japanese government funds 22 percent of the private sector's R&D—only half of the U.S. government's investment. This permits a more market-oriented investment of R&D resources, which certainly benefits industry.

*31. Competitive spirit.*   Japanese industry functions in a more consumer-oriented environment than does U.S. industry. Japan's small defense budget effectively subtracts military contracts from industries' priority considerations, and competition for the consumer's approval increases. In an intensely competitive environment, one has to try harder to win market shares. This stimulates quality, since quality wins customers, as car sales prove.

*32. Self-mation.*   This unique development of the Japanese auto industry allows manufacturers to prevent an automated line from getting out of adjustment and putting out a series of unsatisfactory parts. Self-mation involves a sensor which, when a machine begins making parts that are out of tolerance or defective, halts the machine and calls attention to the error.

*33. Candor and consensus management.*   Perhaps one of the most revealing observations in my interviews with Japanese industrialists is the candor they display in giving credit where credit is due (for example, quality assurance lessons from Deming, Juran, and Feigenbaum). They are equally candid in admitting that theirs is, by and large, a management by consensus—total involvement of management in making decisions affecting product or production. Workers participate through quality circles.

*34. Just-in-time (JIT) inventory.*   Japanese dedication to quality has bought them the additional advantage of low inventories, which reduce capital investments in materials, storage space, material handling equipment, and labor. Toyota boasts of a two-hour inventory. The Sony factory in Ichinomiya claims that suppliers' trucks roll in every 90 minutes to keep up with a production rate of one Trinitron color TV or VCR every six seconds. This requires an excellent understanding between Sony and its suppliers. As of 1992, JUSE reports that JIT is being reduced for some critical reasons, including hardship on suppliers, increase in traffic snarls, and pollution!

*35. Supplier quality.*   Just-in-time inventory is impossible without an assurance that suppliers can produce quality goods. The every-90-minute appearance of suppliers' trucks is meaningless if the trucks are forced to do double duty, returning defective merchandise to the suppliers. No manufacturer can maintain a two-hour inventory if the next supply run may contain 10 percent unusable materials.

Failure to maintain the buyer's standard of quality generally means failure of the supplier's business—certainly it ends the supplier's relationship with that buyer.

*36. Quality standards.*   Zero defects is the unwritten but well-understood quality standard of Japanese industry. At a Sony factory in 1982, one could see a color TV that had been operating eight hours a day for over 37,000 operating hours with no adjustments or repairs, and was still producing an acceptable picture. The industry standard is 10,000 hours.

*37. Trading companies.*   Quality is also stimulated by new markets, and Japanese trading companies provide this stimulus to industry. In a constant search for resources, the trading companies pave the way to barter manufactured goods for needed resources. Hard currency comes from countries such as the United States. This system gives Japanese industry the best of all worlds—new business in cash-poor markets and needed resources and dollar markets where quality is important. Sears, Roebuck began such a trading company in America; regrettably, it did not survive.

*38. Line-stop authority.*   In Toyota plants, every worker station has a line-stop button or switch. Each worker is authorized to stop the production line if something goes awry. The worker does not fear reprisal for interrupting production. The point is patently clear: Quality transcends production schedules.

*39. Venture capital from savings.*    The Japanese save more than four times as much as we Americans do, according to the Savings Trend Survey. The average savings rate of all Japanese families was 15.9 percent as of December 1991, although in households where each member worked, the rate was 16.2 percent. An average working family of four has the equivalent of a year's wages in savings. When bonus times roll around, about 35 percent of each bonus is put into savings for a rainy-day need or that big yen purchase that exceeds normal cash flow. As a result of this thriftiness, there is adequate venture capital in Japan for modernization, expansion, and new starts. The first two contribute substantially to quality.

*40. Face-saving and peer pressure.*    Identification with firm and product makes each worker his or her own best quality standard. At Nissan, for instance, the quality people are at the end of the production line for final acceptance. Production workers perform in-process checks. They are responsible for ensuring that their own operations are done properly, but they also check the operation just previous to their stations. It is easy to see the peer pressure of having a production line colleague call attention to an inadequately performed operation.

*41. Constant improvement.*    As Deming is quick to point out, the only acceptable quality standard is one of constant improvement of process and product. The Japanese are avid practitioners of this philosophy.

At Nitsuko, a modest-sized manufacturer and assembler of telephone equipment, a sign—in both Japanese and English—prominently displayed in the production area advises, "The first requirement of the job is to have an inquiring mind." Thinking is not only allowed, it's encouraged. T. Fuji, the managing director, says, "We are not selling telephone equipment. We are selling quality." This is the essence of competitiveness.

*42. Customer satisfaction.*    The customer—a flesh-and-blood human with tastes and distastes, not a faceless, formless impersonal market—is another important aspect of Japanese success. The Japanese understand fully the Golden Rule of business: "He who has the gold, rules." Customers, whether prime contractors, people on the production line, or the ultimate consumers, are of constant concern to the Japanese. What are their tastes? How can we innovate to pique their curiosity about our product? How can we assure that our product is going to give trouble-free service far beyond the warranty period? How can we be responsive to the customer when a breakdown occurs? From design and production to packaging, the Japanese pay attention to detail for the customer's benefit.

*43. Plant exists for employees' benefit.*   In a U.S. survey, 500 executives were asked their most important responsibilities. Customer satisfaction ranked fifth. Workers' welfare was seventh. By comparison, at Tokyo Juki, a manufacturer of commercial sewing machines, office equipment, computers, and tailoring and commercial cleaning equipment, President Takeo Yamaoka states, "Our business exists for the workers—to provide them jobs and fulfillment in life." This is not to imply that customers are unimportant to Yamaoka. On the contrary, he understands that quality products that give competitive market advantage can be produced only by employees who feel they are more than clock numbers.

*44. Directors chosen from within company.*   Japanese directors are normally chosen from inside the organization. In U.S. companies, most directors originate from outside the corporate structure. While this may inject a degree of objectivity and fresh innovation into the boardroom, it is unlikely to provide a detailed understanding and experience of the business at the decision-making level.

*45. Nommunication.*   Here's an example of the synergism that results when workers identify with one another and their company. "Nommunication," Noguchi of JUSE explains, "is what takes place when Japanese workers and management meet at the local bar or restaurant to relax, have a few beers or sake, and discuss their business. It creates a sort of after-hours quality circle where problems, solutions, and new ideas are discussed."

*46. Job rotation.*   U.S. unions have doggedly insisted on members working only within their narrow disciplines. In Japan, workers are rotated to different jobs with their unions' blessings. This gives management wide latitude in dealing with peaks and valleys caused by a changing market. This approach to job assignments is being effectively used in the United States by Nissan in Smyrna, Tennessee. Workers there increase their earnings in proportion to their ability to do different jobs. When expected resignations, death, retirement, or sickness occur, there is no question of having in-house talent to continue production without a hiccup.

*47. Suggestion program.*   In America, some suggestion boxes attract industrious spiders to build cobwebs and collect dust. In Japan, suggestion systems stimulate a harvest of ideas generated by workers. In 1991 some 7 million suggestions were submitted by those most capable of seeing flaws in their manufacturing systems. Fuji Electric boasts of one employee who submitted 5000 suggestions in one year. This is unusual, no question, but is indicative of the enthusiasm and value of the Japanese approach to using in-house brain power. Recognition, reward (though token at times), and prompt processing and feedback are the keys to the success of their programs. Long delays in feedback, petty jealousies and envy on the part of the reviewing team, and penurious payoffs are all symptoms of the illness in the U.S. system.

*48. Favorable environment.*   Does the work environment make any difference in productivity? Without question. It affects the attitude people maintain about their jobs, their productivity, and the quality of their work. Cleanliness, orderliness of storage and production flow, lighting and sound levels, and company uniforms, jackets, and caps, all make employees feel valued. In plants where a combination of poor lighting, lack of floor space, lack of cleanliness, and disorderliness make the place resemble a dungeon, workers are demotivated and unproductive.

*49. Utilization of managerial engineering techniques.*   Can management use the same disciplined techniques of engineers? Yes. Ryuji Fukuda, one of Japan's most sought-after consultants in the United States and Europe, has written a book that should be must reading on the senior manager's list. Titled *Managerial Engineering* and published by Productivity Press, it approaches management as a discipline that can be structured and performed in much the same manner that engineers approach problem solving or technological advances. Reactive management does not foster competitiveness. To regain leadership, we must be proactive, use all our resources, anticipate problems, and prevent their occurrence. Is it possible to achieve this? It's possible and necessary. Reaction isn't management.

*50. Company loyalty.*   Many mistakenly believe that company loyalty is achieved by the much-publicized Japanese company exercises, motto repetition, or singing. It goes much deeper and broader. It consists of a working relationship in which workers recognize that the company is truly concerned, not only about the customer and the product, but about them.

Bonuses, lifetime employment, working conditions, quality circles, suggestion programs, equipment, training, recognition—all of these build employee loyalty. They allow a worker to say, "I am worth something to my employer. I am not just a clock number to be laid off when the economy is in a downturn. I am a valued employee whose opinions are not only sought, but whose suggestions, whether they be individually generated or corporately derived in a quality circle, are important to the welfare and competitive success of this company. This company is me, and I am the difference I make in whatever I do. I must never be guilty of giving my company less than my best efforts."

*51. Banks vs. individuals as stockholders or financiers.*   Money to begin, to expand, to grow is an important factor of quality. Unfortunately, U.S. management often believes stockholders are after short-term gains instead of what the investor actually would prefer, steady, long-term growth. In Japan, most large companies are financed by banks and other financial institutions, and these institutions recognize that a well-founded, visionary business ensures not only return and long-term gains, but the opportunity for an investment bonanza. If U.S. businesses would assure investors that they are in the market for the long run, those investors might not feel inclined to seek short-term gains.

*52. Cost consciousness.*   What's our production cost and how does it compare with our competitor's cost? The Japanese are big spenders in their marketing efforts, but they also watch the cost of doing business, recognizing that this has a great impact on profitability. Being as resource-poor as they are, they are also sensitive to waste in their raw materials and administrative expenses.

*53. Successful management of change.*   U.S. businesses have difficulty managing change. Mergers, market perturbations, takeovers, economic downturns, strikes, product change, customer dissatisfaction, natural disasters, and the like upset the norm. We enjoy the comfort that routines afford.

When change is the result of careful planning, it will normally result in acceptance and success. A Japanese market entrance is generally the result of studied research, careful evaluation, and resource support that is willing to take a loss until the venture can get a strong grip on the market. Too often, U.S. firms wait until buggies are obsolete before stopping buggy whip production. We fail to read signs that indicate a changing market and to react. MITI helps Japanese industry keep an eye open for opportunities and supports industries that have the leadership and motivation to pursue such initiatives.

*54. Personnel selection based on potential.*   Few question that people are the single most important element in quality; yet, U.S. hiring practices are superficial and shallow. Tokyo Juki President Takeo Yamaoka says, "Selection of personnel is the most important phase of quality. We screen people very carefully and base our selection on two principle criteria: First, does the person really want to work for Tokyo Juki? Second, what is the applicant's potential? We are interested in what an applicant has achieved, but we feel his or her potential is much more important. How can an employee grow with us? What can he or she contribute?"

This philosophy was echoed by Marvin Runyon, the first president of Nissan America, subsequently chief of the Tennessee Valley Authority, and currently head of the U.S. Postal Service: "We are interested only in people who want to identify on a long-term basis with Nissan America. After a very careful screening and training period, the prospective employee interviews with the line supervisor he or she will work for. Then, if the new hire doesn't work out, human resources can't be blamed."

*55. Contribution to society.*   The Japanese feel an obligation to their society. They credit it with enabling them to succeed. In the United States, we often take our society, as well as our people, very much for granted. Japanese managers believe that business exists to contribute to society, not to exploit it.

The seriousness of this obligation was demonstrated in the early 1980s by a Japanese skipper who committed suicide because his ship got caught in a storm that severely damaged his cargo of new cars. He felt he had failed to live up to his responsibility. Even more recently, when a Japanese 747 lost a vertical stabilizer, causing it to crash with a loss of 520 lives, the chairman of the airline resigned. In the United States, companies dump toxic waste indiscriminately, violate safety procedures, and release poisonous gases with little concern except to wonder how their firms will survive.

*56. Timing (or just plain luck).*   Taiichi Ohno, originator of Toyota's JIT inventory system, says the biggest contributors to Toyota's success are: "luck and timing. When the gas crisis came, we had a product ready to take advantage of the market. It was a matter of timing!"

Of course, timing had little to do with Japan's success in the electronic watch, optics, and camera fields—that was pure quality.

*57. Market research.*   Fuji film has been on the market for many years, but it was not until the 1984 Olympics that it became readily available everywhere. Fuji had targeted that event for its serious market entry, and the firm heavily advertised Fuji as the official film of the 1984 Olympics. It had determined that Kodak—long the predominant film in the market—was vulnerable to challenge, and, groundwork done, Fuji made its move.

*58. Investment of profits.*   Plowing profits into a business to enhance its competitiveness makes good sense. Too often, however, the temptation to acquire new businesses—about which we know little, but which appear to diversify us—overwhelm us. At a time when competitive advantage did not depend on a discriminating customer, diversification might have been a proper decision. However, the times now dictate that we provide whatever resources are necessary to make changes, improve performance, and offer a product that will win the customer's loyalty. The Japanese operate on this premise; Komatsu is a case in point. When faced with severe competition from Caterpillar, Komatsu focused on and invested in quality, and now its sales centers are a common sight on Caterpillar's home turf in the United States.

*59. Published policy.*   Policy is the published heartbeat of any organization. This written document tells management and workers what the business is and what is expected of employees; it also establishes the customer's preeminent status. It is signed by the CEO and promulgated in such a manner that all hands understand its contents and application to them. It is not an optional directive. It is the *word*.

Too often U.S. companies fail to publish a quality policy, expecting people to intuitively understand what is desired. This can be a fatal omission.

Japanese management establishes standards of expected behavior, productivity, and quality. Then they audit the results closely enough to ensure accountability of the individual.

*60. Importance of the individual.*   The importance of the people has been alluded to a number of times in this chapter. If there is one preeminent rung in the Japanese success ladder, it has to be their true concern for people. Japanese concern isn't superficial or supercilious. The mere image of concern never nurtures identification with or loyalty toward the corporation. It produces clock-and-boss watchers whose definition of *good enough* is "anything I can get away with." It produces subordinates who never tell it like it is. They say what the boss will accept. Are people important to the Japanese executive? In successful companies, they are, without exception.

How many rungs are transferable? At least 55 of the 60 can be adapted by U.S. industry—some more easily than others—but in time, all contributing to our enhanced quality. The five out of reach are:

4. *Ethnic homogeneity of work force*   For obvious reasons;
8. *Economic challenge*   Blessed with land and natural resources, the United States has many decades before resource scarcity will be a problem;
9. *Cultural proclivity for attention to detail*   Japan's limited space and resources encourage attention to detail; American surplus discourages it;
23. *Resource limitation*   Cannot be a motivator for the foreseeable future; and
33. *Consensus management*   When we elect or appoint a president or board chair, we expect that person to make decisions and want to hold them accountable.

## WHAT IS REQUIRED?

The question remains, what is required to adapt Japan's positive forces to American industry and to our population's psyche? The answer lies in *leadership*—leadership, in both government and industry, that sets goals, motivates, and leads by example. This issue is detailed in chapter 13.

Visits to Japan to witness the effect of leadership on quality and productivity are justified, but only to the degree that the trip excites the sensitivities and improves understanding of *why* the Japanese have achieved worldwide successes in the marketplace and quality, and *how* American approaches to management can change to achieve similar successes.

# 7 KOREA: THE AWAKENING GIANT

Tokyo's international airport at Narita now resembles America's corporate convention center, but within the next five years might well shift to Kimpo in Seoul, Korea. Many of the ingredients tht contributed to our own industrial downfall appear to be present in Japan's economy: a growing budget deficit that will inevitably require an increase in taxes (a value-aded tax is a leading contender), inflation, and affluence—all are factors that may put a damper on Japan's industrial ardor.

Korea, on the other hand, has a labor pay scale that will permit it to compete for markets in any area for many years to come. Also, Korean workers seem indefatigable, logging six- and seven-day work weeks and 10- to 12-hour work days. Vacations? "No vacation," said one Korean executive, "Plenty of time off for Christmas, funerals, Liberation Day, and Buddha's birthday." This work ethic is a key building block in any market takeover.

## THE LUXURY OF REWORK

The Daewoo Shipbuilding and Heavy Machinery (DSHM) shipyard in Okpo is impressive. The dry dock measures 530 x 131 x 14.5 meters and can accommodate a 1 million deadweight-ton (DWT) vessel. It can be separated into three sections to fit various needs. A 900-ton traveling Goliath crane (aptly named) spans the 131-meter width of the dock. On a typical day, the dock's three sections might be loaded with seven semisubmersible drilling rigs (each 260 x 200 x 116 feet), a 140,000 DWT bulk

**Author's note:** Some of the statistics presented in this chapter are those I gathered on my trips to Korea in the early and late 1980s. When it was possible to update them I did so. However, I left many of my original statistics intact because they still communicate the Korean success story.

carrier, two 17,500 DWT product carriers, a barge-mounted seawater treatment plant, and a back-up drilling rig.

This dock has all the facilities and equipment for a world-class shipbuilding and heavy machinery fabrication source. The facilities are woefully underutilized (no doubt occasioned by the worldwide cutback in shipbuilding), but no expense has been spared in making Daewoo one of the most competitive shipyards in the world, with TQC and quality circles playing significant roles. The 170 organized circles generate their own agendas, and final evaluation of ideas that cross departmental lines are made at the headquarters level.

A strong quality policy prefaces the rather substantial quality manual. It concludes with the following: "The systems and procedures contained in our QA program are mandatory . . . deviations will not be tolerated."

Unfortunately, there is no apparent system for collecting nonconformance data, without which there is no way to ensure process control. One must discover where errors and deviations are being generated. Daewoo's answer is, "*We do it over* as often as necessary to satisfy the customer." Daewoo can afford that attitude only as long as the 1991 labor rate of $5.60 per hour holds. If worker expectations grow, a true system approach to quality control will become mandatory.

Daewoo has another potential weak spot in its quality program: The quality organization is fragmented, and there's a quality system at only one of Daewoo's major yard divisions. (This weakness is also present in some large U.S. corporations.)


## SHOE QUALITY

Kukji Corporation turns out 200,000 pairs of shoes a day. These range from Nike tennis shoes and joggers to boots and overshoes. Each day of the six-day week consists of $10\frac{1}{2}$ hours including an hour for lunch and two half-hour coffee breaks to relieve the tension of production line work. While there is little automation in this very labor-intensive plant, quality is excellent. There is less than 0.01 percent scrap, and that is burned as fuel. Rejects and returns from customers amount to 0.5 percent. These low scrap and reject rates are attributable to two factors: the high quality standards established by Kukji for its workers, and tough statistical sampling of shoes during production. New product lines are also tested rigorously.

## Kukji and Education

About 3000 of Kukji's 18,000-person work force are teenage females who receive $100 a month, room and board, and an opportunity to go to school after work. School is considered a real dividend for these girls, who would not otherwise have this opportunity for education. Regular production workers receive from $150 to $250 a month for their efforts. At the high end, this represents less than $1.50 an hour. There is also a bonus system that included a month's pay at the lunar New Year and a similar bonus on National Thanksgiving Day.

## POSCO

The Pohang Iron and Steel (POSCO), located in Pohang, is so clean and orderly that it's difficult to believe it is the world's sixth largest operating steel plant. This 2200-acre plant has its own port, three steel and four blast furnaces, and a production force of 14,500.

Even though POSCO imports 96 percent of its ore and 100 percent of its coal, this $3.6 billion complex in 1981 produced the most inexpensive steel in the free world—$422 per long ton compared to $560–600 for Japanese steel and $800 for American steel. POSCO's capital investment was repaid by 1988. Such rapid loan repayment is achievable only by producing a competitive product. The fringe benefit is the loan-eligible image it projects. Capital investment by banks, not stockholders, is an advantage.

## Quality's Role

Quality performance at POSCO is meticulously recorded, as is analysis of results. For example, in 1973, it took 550 kilograms of coke to produce a long ton of steel. That figure has since been cut to 477–480 kilograms. In 1973, 50 kilograms of oil injection was required; by 1983, POSCO was an oilless operation.

During my visit, a total of 1900 quality circles operated to identify manufacturing quality and productivity problems and correct them. These circles operate in administration, sales, and production departments. Top management sets goals and work standards and monitors their implementation and support.

**Worker Job Satisfaction**
Since Pohang is somewhat remote from Seoul, POSCO has invested in 2600 housing units to accommodate 4346 families and bachelor dorms for another 4031 workers. Included are schools to ensure workers' children ample preparation for the extremely difficult college entrance exams. Houses are purchased through interest-free loans from POSCO. There are no unions, since workers' committees negotiate any requirements or misunderstandings with management. These management-labor councils meet monthly.

Bonuses of one month's salary are paid quarterly to POSCO's labor force. If business is above average, bonuses are increased to total six months of wages.

**Introductory Briefings for Visits**
The Japanese are not the only people from the western rim of the Pacific basin who visit abroad and take notes; the Koreans have done so, too. POSCO provides visitors an introductory briefing that includes slides and a Harvard-accented narrative that would do any major U.S. corporation proud. POSCO Executive Vice President Intaek Kim's rapid recitation of company statistics identifies him as a man who is involved in details. Expansion plans include a new plant in Gwangyang, on the southern tip of Korea. Preparation of the construction site began in September 1982, and was completed in October 1985 with the first stage of the mill begun in March of 1985 and completed in May of 1987. Subsequent stages were completed in July 1988, March 1989, and December 1990.

## SAMSUNG GROUP

The literal translation of Samsung is *three stars*. Samsung Electronic Company's symbol is a tri-star that stands for quality, technology, and good service. What could better epitomize a customer's desires? This obviously accounts for the Samsung Group's financial growth from 3.0 percent of Korea's GNP in 1974 to 7.9 percent in 1981. Samsung, in the Kyungri-Do area of Seoul, is among the top 30 electronic-products plants in the world. Products range from linear integrated circuit boards to refrigerators. In product range and production capability, Samsung Electronics is impressive. The firm's innovative use of technology disputes the concept that Japan and Korea produce nothing original.

## Worker Quality Audit

All 15,000 Samsung personnel, regardless of assignment, receive formal training before being assigned to production. Once there, they're exposed to a combination of peer pressure and supervisor monitoring, which serve as motivation for quality work. Some workers get flags by their work stations. A yellow flag means the worker has made one significant mistake in assembly; a red flag indicates two. If a third one occurs, the employee is moved into a less-demanding job. Reassignment, not firing, is management's reaction to errors. This supports worker identification with the company and prevents the loss of training investment.

## Lots of Rework, No Scrap

Samsung is one of the few Korean businesses that have a significant system for documenting nonconformance. Executive Managing Director Y. M. Jung indicates that about 10 percent of the color TVs Samsung produces require some degree of rework. This is about the same as rework rates at Sony in Japan. Of 1800 refrigerators produced by Samsung, some 5 percent required rework. There was no scrap generated in either the TV or refrigerator line. The microwave oven line—Samsung claims to have about 13 percent of the U.S. market—had 3 percent to 4 percent rework. Zero defects is the quality goal throughout the organization. Quality programs center around technology, supplier control, and personnel motivation.

## Young Work Force

The average age of workers at Samsung is 20, and their annual bonuses, based on longevity, averages about four months' pay. There is no union, but, as with POSCO, there is a management-labor council where elected workers meet with management to settle differences. Quality circles number between 400 and 500. They meet weekly on their own initiative. These circles set their own goals. When one set of goals is met, new goals are established. Total quality control is a way of life at Samsung.

## Quality of Life: Company Policy

At Samsung, the group chairperson has established a three-point corporate policy: to serve Korea through business, to put human resources above material, and to require efficient management. Samsung Electronics also has a four-point policy that encourages quality in work life: cultivate mutual respect of all Samsung employees, create vitality throughout the organization, create an atmosphere of mutual trust, and complete all work to perfection.

It is easy to see why Samsung has been awarded the Korean Presidential Award for Quality.

## ORIENTAL PRECISION COMPANY

Oriental Precision Company (OPC) manufactures telecommunications and computer peripherals, portable field radio transceivers, sonobuoys, traffic control systems, and other products. The firm has a reliability testing system second to none. Here is a manufacturer confident enough of its design and manufacturing system to subject the product to shock and drop tests that truly duplicate the likely treatment the communication gear will receive on the battlefield.

Very education-minded, OPC is a major funder of Dae-Yeu Technical College, a local school that trains, among others, OPC personnel.

### Sound Organization

Kwang Hyun Kim, a retired general of the Republic of Korea Army, is president of OPC. He also identifies himself as the one responsible for quality control at OPC. "The QC director reports directly to me, as it must be," he says.

More than 190 quality circles involve over 3000 employees. Oriental Precision Company's three quality thrusts are ensuring that employees are adequately trained and motivated, ensuring that materials and supplier components meet customer specs, and checking final product to ensure that it meets customer expectations. The second point is particularly important, since OPC is assembly oriented, fabricating only 20 percent of its components.

## GOLD STAR GUMI

In a remote southeastern region of Korea is Gold Star Gumi, a missile overhaul facility. The work spaces, even during full operation, are operating-room clean. Accurate rework figures for each type of missile are recorded: 4.6 percent rework on the Sidewinder, 5 percent on the I Hawk, and 3 percent on the Vulcan.

Intraplant competition spurs Gumi's more than 60 quality circles to see which circle can generate the most significant ideas for improvement of quality or productivity. There is no union—only a management-labor council—and biannual bonuses amount to four and one-half months' pay (equivalent to a total of nine months' pay) paid out twice a year. Company housing and night school assistance foster company identity and support the theory that training and education promote quality and productivity.

## KOREAN STANDARDS ASSOCIATION

The Korean Standards Association (KSA), created in 1962, pursues much the same path as JUSE. In 1971, it was designated as the training institute for certified quality engineers, and in 1977, it was named national headquarters for promotion of quality circles.

As of 1992, KSA was headed by Suhn Hong Kim, also president of KIA Motors. KSA consists of 3482 member companies and has published over 8560 standards. In 1991 there were 105,000 graduates of KSA-sponsored courses (including home-study courses, regular KSA courses, and courses held at companies). KSA publishes five periodicals and numerous quality books and training aids. Nearly 400 qualified experts in the field of quality provide consulting and training services. KSA claims that 20 percent of all workers in Korean industry are members of the country's 34,716 quality circles.

Like JUSE, KSA's strength lies in the fact that its membership consists of firms, not individuals. As a result, it can generate the financial backing and corporate interest in quality so essential for success of such a venture. Neither government action nor support from the quality community can cause such an organization to be formed in the United States. Top management of U.S. corporations must bring this about. The need does exist.

## WHAT CAN WE LEARN FROM KOREA?

Korea is an awakening industrial giant to be reckoned with in the near future. Survivors of a long and seesaw war on their homeland, Koreans have demonstrated a singleness of purpose that demonstrates staying power. They have done a remarkable job of recovering from war and now—enthusiastic and willing to work—are entering the arena of world industrial competition. Taking a cue from their Japanese neighbor's success, they recognize that the key to success is quality.

Korea has several advantages over the United States and Europe. Some we can overcome with sufficient effort, others we cannot. One of the Korean advantages that won't disappear in the near future is its low cost of labor. The wage difference may shrink over time, but the traditional subsistence-level economy of Korea will continue to give Korean producers an edge. (An interesting point: There are no unemployment benefits in Korea. Families are expected to take care of their own.)

### Education
While the Japanese focus on education is lauded in the Western world, Korea surpasses the Japanese in motivation and system. Japanese competition for admission to colleges and universities is intense, but once there, some students coast. Not so in Korea. Although competition for college entry is as keen in Korea as it is in Japan, once in school, freshmen and sophomores suffer significant attrition. Koreans believe that college is a place to learn and enhance one's value to the nation—not a social club at which to cultivate future business friends. This education does not cease once the student is out of technical school or college, but continues in off hours in one's chosen field.

### Work Ethic
Koreans are raised with the personal philosophy that hard work makes the difference. Instead of constantly looking for ways to shorten their work hours, days, or weeks, they believe that God gave humanity energy and strength to conquer both self-generated problems and those occurring naturally. Success, not leisure time, is the goal of a Korean, and success is measured by one's contribution to society. Koreans have no need for unions, for both management and labor have been weaned on the same work ethic. They can communicate with one another because they do not feel the need for a third party.

Management understands the contribution of labor as being the key to success and survival. Labor, accordingly, recognizes the contribution of management in providing capital, technology, and direction. It's a partnership arrangement rather than an adversarial one.

Bonuses, company housing, schools, and recognition are the appropriate Korean ways for management to recognize labor's contribution. Likewise, labor feels that an honest day's work is what an employer is entitled to and strives earnestly to provide it.

Americans were born, and flourished, with the same understanding. But, since we've achieved success, we appear to have lost touch with honest, basic human relationships and worth.

### Quality

Korean workers and managers recognize that consumers want quality *and value*. At the moment, constant, tedious rework is the means Koreans use to achieve that quality. But, having shown the capability to achieve, Koreans will soon learn that process control can give them an even greater edge in the international marketplace.

## THE LESSON

Anyone who reads labels knows the incursions Korea has already made in the areas of clothing, textiles, and shoes. "Made in Korea" does not signify inferior quality as "Made in Japan" did in the 1950s. Koreans have looked at Japan—their ancient conqueror and foe—and emulated its approach to quality.

The United States must analyze the factors that have contributed to Korea's success and adopt them. There are markets enough for all if we just take the trouble to develop them.

# 8 ESSENTIAL ELEMENTS OF EXCELLENCE

There are eight elements that top management can use as a basic starting point in evaluating the focus that the company's quality manager has established. Let's look at each area.

## QUALITY TEAMS

Quality teams created by edict may be productive because they sense the confidence management has in the quality system. First of all, do you have a quality team, or groups that resemble quality circles? If so, how many and how often do they meet? Do they meet on company time? Are they voluntary? Who's in charge, and what kind of agenda are they working from?

What's in it for the participant? Obviously, the longevity and prosperity of the company is one commonly shared benefit, but is that all? How about educational and cultural benefits? Have they been considered and advertised to the participants as benefits?

What do you expect out of them and how will they document achievements? Do you have a reward and recognition system that is realistically based on cost avoidance, company savings, or greater profitability from increased productivity? Are the teams goal oriented and of manageable size? Does the team concept extend across disciplines? Did you begin the quality team process with a steering group to test the idea? If so, have patience and wait for the dividends to arrive.

## PROCESS CONTROL

For many years, artificers felt a personal responsibility for the quality of their work. They identified with quality by putting their "mark" on their products. If only one producer existed in the area, it was obvious who was accountable for the goods. Industrialization, mass production, and end-item inspection have eradicated that scene. Complexity, sophistication, and quantity of products have made direct accountability and identification unfeasible. Now, we must control and process to guarantee quality.

Process control begins with the planning stage. It requires close interface with your customer and your design department during product formulation. The next step is determining what procedures will be used for process control of design, production, and quality. The best set of procedures is useless if it isn't understood and implemented by each worker.

To many, process control means no more inspection. But any new product will require at least a first-article inspection to ensure it meets specs, followed by a statistically sound spot-check thereafter. Defects uncovered as a result of these checks must be thoroughly analyzed to determine where and why the quality breakdown occurred. Control charts with upper and lower control limits must be established and monitored.

## CORRECTIVE ACTION

Without corrective action, process control breaks down. People responsible for defects must be advised and redirected to preclude repetition of the error. Corrective action must be a team effort that includes design, engineering, production, and quality. If it involves purchased goods, it should include purchasing and the responsible supplier. It is essential that the corrective action have the ownership of all involved. Once the problem is analyzed and an acceptable solution has been formulated, follow-up is necessary to assess the validity of the fix. If the problem has not been solved, the process goes back to the drawing board.

## FACILITATION

The best training program and the most advanced engineering and design assets will avail little if your people are working with obsolete or inadequate equipment, a lack of floor space, or poor production flow layout. An efficient material control system and material requirements plan, an appropriate degree of automation, and an industrial environment that supports your quality standards are all essential elements of an acceptable facilitation plan.

One can't determine adherence to customer specifications without accurate measurement. How accurate is your gaging instrumentation? The sophistication in this phase of process control gives little excuse for ever having problems here. However, the best, most-sophisticated measurement system is useless without an effective calibration system with a built-in audit safeguard.

Facilitation also calls for qualified supervisors who spend time on the shop floor—not in their comfortable cubbyholes. Most workers will consult a supervisor when questions or problems arise, but not if that supervisor is inaccessible.

An often overlooked adjunct to facilitation is employees' support and recreational facilities. Decent and adequately equipped restrooms, lounges, and eating facilities are not luxuries in today's society. They are expected. They help identify a company that cares about its employees. The cost is minimal when compared to the potential payback.


## TRAINING

Training is an exceedingly important factor in achieving high quality standards. For less complex operations, hands-on training may suffice, but, for best results, formal training is desirable. This is particularly true when significant modernization or updating occurs.

One of the best insurance policies against demoralizing and quality-costly layoffs is to institute cross-skill training. Then, when sickness, vacation, or a market valley occurs, workers can be shifted to meet the skill demand. Marvin Runyon, former president and general manager of Nissan America, did this at Nissan's Smyrna, Tennessee, plant. Workers who are cross-trained at this plant are paid at a higher scale than those who are not, and a slow-down on the production line never occurs due to a lack of skill.

Technology updates for supervisors and management are also important to nurture an attitude of constant improvement within your organization. The Japanese have discovered that mid-life training at age 45 does wonders in rejuvenating middle- and upper-level management.

## QUALIFICATION/CERTIFICATION PROGRAMS

Qualification and certification programs with regularly scheduled audits ensure that personnel are indeed qualified. Such programs are essential if the audited skills are extremely technical or exotic.

## QUALITY STANDARDS

There are four gages by which to evaluate the realistic value of quality standards. First, they must be definable. If it is zero defects you'd like to establish as your standard, by all means do so. Perhaps you prefer Deming's approach of constant improvement. Whatever the goal, have it clearly understood that this is *the* acceptable goal for everyone. Second, ensure that your people understand your published quality standard. Be certain that this standard is measurable (gage three). If you have not opted for a zero defects standard, you should define as gage four the degree of nonconformance you are willing to accept. A base line is necessary to determine a starting point from which to measure progress. If you can't measure it, you can't manage it.

Recognize or reward workers who achieve the standard. If the standard has been jointly established by management and nonmanagement, the probability of its acceptance is increased a hundredfold. If your standard had been established as less than zero defects, steadily raise the goals, just as you would in training a hurdler or high-jumper.

W. Somerset Maugham, the great English novelist, is quoted as having said, "It's a funny thing about life—if you refuse to accept anything but the best, you very often get it." Don't be timid in setting high standards. Your employees will rise to the occasion if you exemplify those same high standards of performance.

Benchmarking is another tool that fits in the quality standards category. What are the *leaders* in the industry doing? Do you know? Do you care? You should, since *they* are the ones who are after your share of the market. After finding out how well they are doing, see if you can find out *what* they are doing to achieve their position. Normally you will discover that they have developed a close kinship with both the *internal* and *external* customers that serves as course direction for their management decisions.

## COMMUNICATION

Quality is largely a matter of effective communication between people. It must first be communicated, understood, and accepted in house. Part of the message must be about the personal satisfaction that quality will give every participant.

Next, communicate quality to your customers via the product or service you produce or provide. "Your product speaks so loudly, I can't hear what your advertising campaign is saying." The Edsel is an example of that truth—customers spoke with their pocketbooks. Buick's boast, "Ask the man who owns one," and Sears', "Satisfaction guaranteed" are long-lasting reminders of the customer satisfaction provided by their products.

It is also essential that stockholders and directors understand what quality means to their investment. Overall product integrity is essential for the reputation of your company and product in the marketplace and industry.

# 9 QUALITY OF LIFE

How important are people to you? Are they to be used only as long as they require a minimum investment of time and money and then let go when they become only marginally profitable or an expense? Do you update employees' technological skills or do you view retraining as a needless cost? Perhaps you say, "We'll hire people fresh out of a technical junior college. They must have been trained on all these new machines and procedures." Are people as important to you as automation or robotics? Do people have a future in your organization, or do you feel their constant wage and fringe increases and noncommensurate productivity increases are unwarranted expenses? Do your employees identify themselves with your company and your products, or is their affiliation with you just another job? Do they, like Teruhisa Tanaka, say the equivalent of "I am NKK and NKK is me"?

Peter Drucker, one of America's foremost management experts, in *Concept of the Corporation*, puts people into a proper context as he writes, "Modern production, and especially modern mass production, is not based on raw materials or gadgets, but on principles of organization . . . not of machines, but of human beings . . . ."[1]

## THE HUMAN ELEMENTS OF QUALITY

One does not experience a successful exposure session, one does not instill workers with a sense of mission, and one does not establish a positive corporate image if management and labor don't function in an atmosphere of mutual respect. Are management and nonmanagement a team in your company, or is there an *us-them* rivalry that prevents everyone from turning out quality? Are the professionals considered to be the elite of the work force, while the molder, pattern maker, the lathe operator, welder, and assembler are necessary evils to be tolerated but not respected?

If the latter is the case, consider where cash flow comes from. From drawings, or from completed product? From management techniques, or from delivered goods? Salaried and hourly workers must cooperate to furnish quality to consumers.

## Leaders and Followers

Leadership is another important human element of quality. It is perhaps the most misunderstood and, thus, poorly taught element in management schools today. Leadership is the thoroughbred that leads the pack to the finish line. Management is the draught horse that dutifully makes the rounds, routinely and profitably delivering beer kegs to customers. This is not to disparage the talents or contributions of managers. They are responsible for ensuring that budgets are met and that the figures on the bottom line are written in black ink. But bear in mind that those figures are primarily the product of the productivity and quality of your line workers! In addition, managers stimulate growth, but seldom do they inspire people to work above self-imposed limitations. That ability to inspire is what leadership is all about: causing people to live beyond their imagined limitations—getting them to reach beyond good enough and discover their true potentials for quality or productivity. It is essential that a good manager also be a good leader if he desires the establishment of a quality culture within his firm.

Equally important in a quality-of-life program is the need for dedicated followers—followers of the sort who can question without being disloyal, those who give their best efforts and inspire others to do likewise. Not everyone can be a leader, but everyone can learn to be a dedicated follower.

*Responsibility and accountability.* Does all responsibility reside on the shoulders of top and middle managers, or has it been distributed throughout the organization? The manager who tries to handle all the details will damage effectiveness as a quality manager. Besides, delegation of responsibility stimulates growth and job satisfaction. It increases self-assurance and pride, making workers feel that their contributions to the firm are important and worthy of their best efforts.

The twin to responsibility is accountability, a leadership characteristic widely neglected in recent decades. Companies fail or lose money, and the decision makers who were paid to know better are quietly reassigned or allowed to float softly on a golden parachute. If we are ever to establish a quality society, we must upgrade the importance of accountability of all hands.

*Goals and self-improvement.* Goals are also important in a quality-of-life program. Are your company goals well known and supported? Did your workers have any input in establishing them? Does everyone believe the goals to be achievable, desirable, and of value to him or her personally? If so, there's a better-than-even chance you will get support for those goals. If they are vague, if they were created in a vacuum, or if they're viewed as unrealistic, your chances of support are greatly reduced.

Self-improvement is a necessity when you consider a quality-of-life program. This can be achieved by in-house sponsored training or education and by motivating people to improve themselves on their own time. The motivation for this must be clearly defined as promotional opportunity within your company.

Obviously, education will also improve an employee's external employment value. But it is up to you to emphasize the employee's opportunity to move up *within* the corporation.

## Team Spirit Is Inspirational

The idea of belonging to a winning team is inspirational and infectious. When the Redskins, Steelers, or Cowboys bring home the Super Bowl trophy, everyone in the hometown suddenly becomes one of the team, and it is hard to resist joining the "We're number one" chant. In industry, it is difficult to be a winner without that team spirit.

## Individual and Corporate Identity

People like to feel that they are important. One way managers can give that feeling is to learn their workers' names. The cost of this employee benefit is zero; the payback is in mutual respect and the increased effort of happy employees.

Of almost equal importance is the employees' identification with their employer. There are three keys to cultivating such an identity lock.

*Encourage interpersonal relationships.* Schedule exposure sessions to update your people on plans, achievements, problems, and potentials, and make yourself available to field their questions. The latter element can be painful because today's worker is not reluctant to dethrone authority. On the other hand, such sessions provide a great catharsis for employees who may need a frustration outlet to restore morale. Restrain your anger, flip answers, biting sarcasm, or the perfect put-down, however tempted you may be to snap back. You are on the firing line to determine just how cool an operator you really are. If you're unsure of the answer to a question or plain don't know, admit it. Promise to find out and get back with an answer. No one knows everything about everything, nor is he or she expected to. These questions may make you aware of areas you should learn more about.

*Sell your people on the importance of what they do.*   As Douglas D. Danforth, emeritus chairman of Westinghouse, once said, "Our performance in the marketplace will be determined by quality as the customer perceives it. It does not matter whether it is product performance, service, competitive pricing, responsiveness to customer needs, or just answering a phone call. Every service you render pushes the enterprise up. Every disservice pushes it down. Too many people think that high quality always carries a high price tag. Wrong."[2]

Is yours an insurance business? Is it just a means of separating people from their money, or does it provide a service people *need* to cope with uncertainties of life and to make provisions for their survivors?

Perhaps you are manufacturing or installing automotive components. Your people must be made to identify their work as important in providing mobility for the public. The job isn't the installation of a right front-disc brake; it's satisfying the public's need for safe and reliable transportation. *That* is a mission that demands a worker's best effort and full attention.

*Project a positive company identity.*   Is it positive? Do people outside of Podunk, where your main (perhaps only) plant is located, know about your company? Corporate identity is second only to the reputation of your products. Corporate image, like product reputation, is built on quality. Both involve close correspondence between real virtue and advertising claims.

Perhaps your corporation is so diversified that its reputation and the reputations of its products have long seemed separate. Be slow to draw that conclusion. Consumers are aware of companies that enjoy long and virtuous reputations. The automobile industry has painfully learned the price one pays for trading the reputation birthright for market indifference.

## FUN IS FUNDAMENTAL TO SUCCESS

Would you rather be doing what you're doing than anything else? If not, why continue?

As Don Farrar, president of Avco Operations, Textron, Inc., often said, "Why is it that we have so little dedication and enthusiasm for efforts on which we spend almost one third of our lives and almost half our waking hours?"

The answer most often is that we're not having fun. Work should be a joy, and it can be if we create an environment that causes people to look forward to work. Following are ideas which both management and nonmanagement associates can use to restore zest and identity to the workplace.

## Universal Contribution

- Develop a positive mental attitude (PMA). If you find you don't approach each day saying, as PMA speaker Ed Foreman[3] does, "It's gonna be a *gooood* day," then move on. Don't spend your life being miserable in your work.
- Get to know your fellow employees. Use your coffee break to extend your opportunity for fellowship and positive influence.
- Consider the future of the company as *your* future. Make it a bright one.
- Give every job that you do your best shot. Don't waste your time on shoddy effort.
- Consider your time as your only unrecyclable treasure. Make it count. Use time wisely.
- Participate in company programs and activities. Join the team and help it make a winning effort.
- Bear in mind, scrap and rework have no reward for the company or you. Do your best to do it right the first time every time.
- When in doubt, ask your supervisor. Don't muddle through because you are too shy or embarrassed to ask for help.
- Identify with the company. It represents not only your livelihood, but your future growth and opportunity.
- Strive for constant improvement as your prime contribution to that winning team to which you belong.
- Demonstrate respect for your subordinates' personalities. They're living, breathing humans who are unique in their responses to stimuli. Learn what evokes a positive response from them.
- Maintain an open channel of communication with superiors and subordinates. Keep everyone informed of what's going on so nobody feels he or she is a "mushroom."
- Know what's going on. Spend time on the shop floor with your eyes and ears open. Manage by walking around.

- Praise in public, reprimand in private. Never miss an opportunity to "catch someone doing something right," as *The One-Minute Manager*[4] advises. If your subordinates are fouled up through either ignorance or indifference, don't hesitate to bring this to their attention, but in private, not before their peers.
- Tangibly demonstrate interest in your subordinates' welfare. If they've got personal problems, take time to counsel or provide a sympathetic ear. So it makes you late getting home from work. Shouldn't their problems be yours if listening helps them become a more responsible and grateful team member?
- Lead by example. Don't expect your people to demonstrate team spirit if you are always knocking your superiors in management. If you are a late-in, early-out supervisor, how can you reprimand tardiness on the part of your people?
- Promote company identity programs. This is essential if you want a winning team.
- Take the drudgery out of work. Make work as much fun as possible for all, yourself included. Encourage humor and interaction on the job.
- Provide an orientation program for all new employees. Where possible, include spouses. They are extremely important in promoting a positive quality-of-life environment.
- Provide formal training for both white- and blue-collar employees. This should include periodic refresher training that updates employees technically and in product awareness.
- Develop a favorable physical environment. Consider cleanliness, orderliness, and appointments in your own office and in other work spaces.
- Provide an environment of job security.
- Develop and implement a plan to stimulate loyalty to the corporation, the division, and the section.
- Identify "up-comers" with great potential and invest the time to develop their potential. Don't promote prematurely, throwing people into positions they're not yet ready to assume.
- Promote from within. Avoid, as much as possible, going outside to fill key slots.
- Develop a good worker reward system as a satisfactory alternative to promotion.
- Provide periodic refresher training for executives.
- Structure bonuses to reward above-and-beyond effort, not just long and faithful service.

## MANAGEMENT'S IMPACT ON QUALITY OF LIFE

There are three principal quality-of-life areas a manager can affect within his or her realm of authority and responsibility: attitude, discipline, and resources. You, as a general manager, are uniquely capable of affecting these areas more than anyone else.

### Attitude Orientation

How can you balance the cost of people and their productivity? The key is attitude orientation.

Without question, the most critical change necessary to achieve a quality culture is the changing of peoples' attitude about what they do. To change attitudes, one must first define quality. Does it mean excellence? To excel? Does quality mean there is none better? Actually, no. It means fulfilling the customer's expectations and having a fitness for use. A Volkswagen can and should represent quality as much as a Rolls Royce, Mercedes, or Jaguar— depending on the taste and purse of the customer. Quality is doing the right thing right, the first time, on time, and achieving value in the buyers' eyes. Concomitantly, there must be profit to the seller, otherwise production capability will soon disappear.

All who have anything to do with design, manufacturing, sales, or service must perceive themselves as owning responsibility for quality. This, together with a performance standard that covers the spectrum of product or service creation, will ensure a mindset that supports your quality culture.

Our complex society is overwhelmed by the negative messages of the news media and is constantly reminded that the nuclear "sword of Damocles" hangs over the human race. It is little wonder that we no longer associate quality with giving our best efforts in all we do. The moral absolutes of the Bible have given way to situational ethics, and the only sin is getting caught. We pay our entertainers on the stage or playing field more than we do our president or legislators, and then wonder why the better-qualified people aren't drawn to run for public office.

Our cynicism regarding basic tenets such as honesty, integrity, and commitment spawns get-by efforts, clock-watching dedication, shoddy work, and litigation for perceived employment bias. Is it any wonder we have a quality problem in this nation?

The attitude problem is not restricted to *them*. It is *us* also. Sensing the possibility of a board's dissatisfaction with our future efforts, or of a hostile takeover, we negotiate golden parachutes into our contracts, giving ourselves a sense of security and reducing our need to be competitive.

We blame others for the problems our company suffers: "Union work rules have ruined the worker." Workers now expect excessive fringe benefits, and they feel no sense of responsibility for judicious use of medical or dental care. Productivity has fallen off and overtime occasioned by rework and repair is creating a real morale problem.

We continue to call in consultants and specialists to identify problems, foregoing the management responsibility that is patently ours. If people are our problem, then it's *our* responsibility to learn how to work with them. If poor morale is killing quality and productivity, management must create an environment that will enhance morale and cause people to feel that coming to work for the ABC Company is the most exciting, challenging, and rewarding thing they can do. Pipe dream? Absolutely not. It is definitely achievable. Later in this chapter you will find a few suggestions on methods.

### Discipline Essential

System discipline is an essential element in exacting efficiency and effectiveness. It is a self-discipline that says, "What *I* do is important to quality." It is much easier to assign others the responsibility for quality and downplay one's own contribution. A quality culture must begin as a conscious responsibility of each individual in the organization.

This discipline must flow from the top and permeate every production process. Statistical quality control must be a way of life in every critical process of the manufacturing procedure. Discipline in design, purchasing, supplier relationships, marketing, and service departments—all must operate within clearly stated rules and regulations that lend discipline and predictability to the system, but that don't stifle creativity, initiative, or innovation.

Organizational discipline is based on every party's recognition of the mutually reinforcing importance of the quality triangle of producer, supplier, and customer. Each makes a vital contribution to the success of any quality improvement process. The supplier provides components and parts that meet assembler/integrator/user requirements on time and on price. The producer manufactures and assembles the product correctly the first time, thereby giving the customer the lowest price, making a profit, and sustaining competitive advantage. The customer, the remaining element of this triad, feeds back approval or disapproval to the producer, providing sufficient detail to allow correction or improvement of the product. Without this feedback, the producer may live in a fool's paradise, believing the product or service is acceptable when, in fact, it is not.

## Resources

An inescapable top management responsibility is the prudent assignment of resources. Of equal truth is the fact that, without resources, little of a positive nature occurs.

But isn't quality free? Yes and no. If we do the right thing right the first time—what we pay our employees for and for which we are paid—and produce an acceptable product or service at the lowest possible cost, then quality is indeed free. However, in a culture that has not yet focused on quality as a way of work life, we need to reform mindsets, and changing a culture is indeed an extensive and expensive undertaking. The alternative, of course, is to fall farther behind in competitiveness.

Perhaps the most critical resource a top manager can supply is time— time to participate actively as the leader in the move to a quality culture in one's organization. It is amazing the effect a manager's active participation in the quality improvement process can have on his or her subordinates. Vice presidents, directors, managers, and first-line supervisors generally take interest in their superior's interests. If a superior's interest is limited to lip service rather than involvement, subordinates' participation will be likewise. Therefore, time is the most valuable contribution a manager can make.

Commitment of resources to provide adequate training and retraining, to provide equipment capable of holding the tolerances your product demands, or to provide efficient office equipment uses your employees' time to best competitive advantage. Are your facilities designed to accommodate your current production or customer schedule? Have you recently checked to ensure your production flow avoids back or cross-tracking as various sequential functions are performed? Have you ignored your industrial engineers' admonitions to expand or update equipment to meet quality and production standards? Have you used the oft-heard excuse, "I can't afford it now. When business gets better, I'll modernize?" You may not remain in a position for business to get better with that attitude.

How about expertise on the shop floor, in design, in engineering, or in marketing? Do you have an executive training program that keeps those functions up to date with the times, technology, and competition? Expertise can be more important than facilities or equipment.

**Recognition**

As a final thought about management's impact on quality of life, how about tangible recognition in the form of gain sharing or bonuses for your employees? After all, are they not responsible for your business success? What motivation do they have for making your business more successful and more competitive? Why not share a piece of the pie? If employees feel they are just making the effort for you, your executive staff, and your shareholders, their effort will be less than if they felt they'd profit from extra effort and care.

Recognition is an important element in any quality-of-life enhancement program. This recognition can be simply walking through the shop area and getting acquainted with the work force. Such a gesture can mean the difference between your success and failure as manager. Recognition can be an all-hands meeting at which a more formal acknowledgment can be made. Or it can be a trophy, a bonus, or a handshake. What it must be is management's acknowledgment of a job well done, commensurate with established quality standards: meaningful recognition.

In all of this, there must be a feeling of mutual trust and respect. Promised rewards and benefits must be honored. If there is any hint of management compromise on either standard or performance evaluation, your program of recognition and reward for performance will disintegrate.

Too often, management and labor have imagined that money is the only recognition—that, in lieu of respect, cash settlements will buy off frazzled nerves, inattention to detail, and adversarial emotions. This bribery fails to produce quality because it fails to produce teamwork, self-respect, or competence. Instead it produces a rift in the day's-work-for-a-day's-pay relationship. It produces a spiraling wage rate and a work force motivated by dollars, not deeds.

**To Change a Culture**

Changing a culture is not easy. Habits, traditions, and mindsets change slowly. Successful culture change requires education, example, and proper recognition. One short training session will not do it. Repetition and reiteration must include not only the *whats* of quality, but also the *whys*. Perhaps the best teaching asset is one's own example of excellence in all activities. An environment of job security helps greatly. A plant that stimulates loyalty to the division or corporation helps create the ownership or identity that will make employee attitudes positive toward what they do.

If you identify comers and assist them to achieve their potential, you'll signal your interest in people, and promoting from within squelches the feeling that everything good comes from the outside. Consider how promoting from within stimulates competition among and effort from those whose loyalty and dedication have already been established. Development of an award system for outstanding workers can be used as a satisfactory alternative to promotion when advancement opportunities stagnate.

Can excellence be achieved in industry today? Can the United States regain its reputation for quality? Absolutely. It requires only *People*, *Resources*, *Identity*, *Dedication*, and *Enthusiasm*. Put them together and they spell PRIDE—pride in workmanship and pride in belonging.

In speaking about how to obtain quality of life, Sir William Osler said, "Live neither in the past nor the future, but let each day's work absorb all your interest, energy, and enthusiasm. The best preparation for tomorrow is to do today's work superbly well."[5]

Amen.

## NOTES

1. Peter F. Drucker, *Concept of the Corporation* (Boston, Mass.: Beacon Press, 1969), 213.

2. Douglas D. Danforth, "Quality Means Doing the Job Right the First Time," *Newsweek*, January 30, 1984, 10.

3. Ed Foreman, President, Executive Development Systems Inc., 14135 Midway Road, Dallas, Tex. 75244.

4. Kenneth Blanchard, Ph.D., and Spencer Johnson, M.D., *The One Minute Manager* (New York, N.Y.: William Morrow & Co., 1981), 85.

5. Harvey Cushing, *Life of Sir William Osler* (Oxford: Clarendon, 1925).

# 10 PROBLEM SOLVING

## IN OR OUT OF HOUSE?

*"There are no problems, only challenges and opportunities."*

John Wayne may never be superseded as an American folk hero. His manly physique, thoughtful drawl, polite respect for women and elders, honesty, open patriotism, and sincerity, not to mention his quick draw and deadly aim, captured the imagination of generation after generation who fantasized him as the person they would most like to be. Unfortunately, generations of managers have emulated The Duke's quick-draw, shoot-from-the-hip style in attempting to solve their companies' more complex problems. "Just bring the varmints to me, and I'll shoot them right out of the saddle. After all, ain't that what I'm hired to do?"

First, it is top management's responsibility to see that technical and professional talent is in place. For this to be effectively implemented, top management must understand what business they are in, the market niche on which they plan to focus, and the market's needs or desires. Often markets can be stimulated, but despite the success of Pet Rocks and Hula Hoops, market stimulation via marketing blitz is not always successful. The consumer appears to be growing wiser as more information becomes available.

Part and parcel of top management's brief is familiarity with the competition. It seems obvious from our dwindling market share and financial losses that American automakers still do not take the competition seriously. Trying to browbeat the Japanese into accepting American autos into their market when we refuse to retool to locate the steering wheel to accommodate

113

Japan's right-hand-drive traffic is a case in point. It is doubtful that Honda, Toyota, and Nissan would have made an impact on the U.S. auto market if they had begun exporting their product with the steering wheel on the right-hand side of the front seat.

Finally, with talent in place, and market and competition understood, top management is still not ready to ascend the podium and, like a confident and competent symphony conductor, orchestrate a successful production. Obviously in many American industries we are far from achieving the needs and desires of our most important element—the customer.

Problem solving must involve everyone in the corporation in some way or another. It cannot be a solo performance. Any manager who is jealous of his subordinates' efforts to make the company a success does not deserve the title. People in corporate life who consider themselves loners aren't qualified to wear white hats.

Managers must recognize talent and have the insight and skill to coordinate that talent to produce a winning team. They must exploit the strengths and versatility of their people to produce the synergy of success. They must have the perception to hire and the guts to fire. They must look at ways to bring out the best in each member of their team. They must downplay rivalries that lead to dissension, but encourage competition that causes people to work beyond themselves. They must raise the bars, so, like Olympic contenders, their team members are not satisfied with equalling records—they strive to break them.

Far too often and for too long, managers have barricaded themselves in their well-appointed offices. They don't know the extent of their organizations' problems, nor have they mobilized their best problem solvers. Their withdrawal has been so complete that the phrase "management by walking around" has recently been regarded as something of a revolutionary concept.

For those who await the identification of a problem by a subordinate while the boss sits on the throne, the wait will be a long one. Not that subordinates deliberately desire to scuttle their own economic survival vessel, it's just that they've learned not to disturb the boss engaged in personal matters in an oak-paneled office. Also, each instance of a bruised and bleeding messenger discourages news bearing.

### Directors As Problem Solvers

It is sometimes assumed that corporate directors can function in place of management as problem solvers. This misses the mark. Directors' contributions lie in the area of approving or disapproving management's decisions about expansion, divestiture, debt increase, election of corporate officers, response to proposals, new product undertakings, reaction to hostile takeover attempts, and the like. They aren't appropriate day-to-day firefighters.

Intelligent managers recognize their own limitations and delegate much of the problem-solving responsibility to their staffs, but they don't subtract themselves from the process. They require problems to be brought to their attention and offer comments or alternatives. In other words, the intelligent manager is neither a lone gun nor one who washes his or her hands of a problem.

### Exploring the Problem-Solving Bank

At Tohoku Nitsuko Ltd., a telephone equipment manufacturing company near Tokyo, a sign reads: "The first rule of the job is to have an inquiring mind." Consider the potential for problem identification such an invitation carries. It welcomes employees to question, among other things, company procedures and policies. Nitsuko increases that potential through an active suggestion program. The benefit of full participation is that the extra problem solvers, as a group, have much more knowledge of plan or production problems than any executive or group of executives can possibly supply.

T. Fuji, managing director of Nitsuko states, "We are not manufacturing telephone equipment, but quality." Quality teams, coupled with well-administered programs, have been a rich source of new ideas and solutions to long-festering problems, and they cement a quality partnership between management and workers.

### The Role of Consultants

If you have neither the talent nor the initiative within your organization to identify or organize the elements of your quality problem, the professional quality consultant can contribute. The solution, however, is yours alone.

The consultant, through structured interaction with *your* people, attempts to identify your quality problem. Be forewarned that most problems originate with management since that is who makes policy and controls resources.

Depending on the consultant's professional experience and persuasion, the package delivered will be the identification of *your* problems. It will draw on *your* suggestions. Perhaps even the solutions will be yours. Surely it will be you who determines and implements recommendations and corrective actions.

If you decide you're ready and willing to address your problems in-house, consider the following eight approaches. They're guaranteed to make you and your team more able.

### ISHIKAWA FISHBONE DIAGRAM

The fishbone approach to problem solving is an interactive exercise that requires a facilitator and is normally worked on during company time by quality circles. Perfected by Kaoru Ishikawa, the fishbone approach is a three-step process.

*Step one.*   Participants identify elements they feel have the most impact on quality. For the sake of illustration, let's consider eight areas: competence, commitment, responsiveness/adaptability, continuous improvement, quality of product, safety, cost/productivity, and market strategy/niche (see Figures 10.1 and 10.2).

*Step two.*   To flesh out the fishbones, we identify elements that fall within each of these areas.

Consider *commitment.* Do employees feel that they have equity in the company? Do they proudly identify with the source of their income? What types of rewards and shared futures do they see? Do these stimulate their commitment to quality?

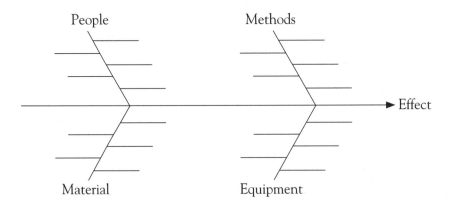

**Figure 10.1.** Model fishbone diagram.

How about *responsiveness* to customers' requirements and adaptability to market changes? Do schedule considerations take precedence over quality? Would a flexible machining system improve responsiveness and market adaptability? To what degree do your marketers have their fingers on the pulse of the market? Are you investing any funds in R&D to *influence* the market?

Is there a recognizable attitude of *continuous improvement* in your organization? If not, how can you create one? What kind of suggestion program do you have, and how active and effective is it? Does customer feedback figure in this element?

Does your *quality system* encompass product delivery, service/tech reps? How about job satisfaction? Does your quality-of-work-life program promote job satisfaction? How do you achieve process control? Is your suppliers' quality assured? Do you have companywide total quality control?

Do you have a functioning *safety* program? Are all hands involved? Do you understand the contributions it makes toward quality, productivity, and quality of work life? Do you publish an accident evaluation to avoid repetitions? What kind of recognitions and rewards do you offer for safety improvement suggestions?

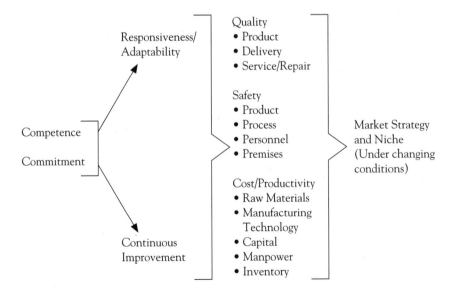

**Figure 10.2.** Elements that have the most impact on quality.

Perhaps the most important area to survey is the cost of *production*. How much is poor design costing in engineering design changes? Is inventory management in hand? Do you have a just-in-time system that relies on vendors to deliver conforming parts when promised? Are nonconformance costs (often mislabeled *cost of quality*) known, and are they acceptably low?

Is quality a factor in your *marketing strategy*? How do your customers compare you with your competitors? Is your firm working on new product innovations? How successful have you been in achieving an acceptance of your quality strategy within your organization? Who does your strategic quality planning? How do you determine market niche? What is your advertising and awareness strategy?

*Step three.* Major problem areas now having been identified and forces listed that have impact on those areas, we now begin the brainstorming phase. Following are two approaches to brainstorming.

## CEDAC

Ryuji Fukuda, the international quality authority mentioned in chapter 6, author of *Managerial Engineering* and consultant to the Meidensha Electric Manufacturing Company, has devised a tool he labels a "cause-and-effect diagram with the addition of cards" (CEDAC). It uses the Ishikawa fishbone diagram and a control chart to display a problem and its scope (see Figure 10.3). Employees are invited to consider a problem and add cards suggesting causes and solutions. Management harvests the cards daily and evaluates them, assuring recognition to all participants. This idea appears to have great merit. For more detail on CEDAC, read Fukuda's excellent text. It's one of the best quality references published.

## BRAINSTORMING, OR NOMINAL GROUP EFFORT

This nominal group effort, labeled brainstorming, is a basic and ad hoc way to uncover available talent and use it in identifying and solving problems. It will boost quality and productivity and provide your workers with the satisfaction and professional growth they deserve. The group can be homogeneous or heterogeneous and can include hourly, salaried, professional, technical, and management personnel.

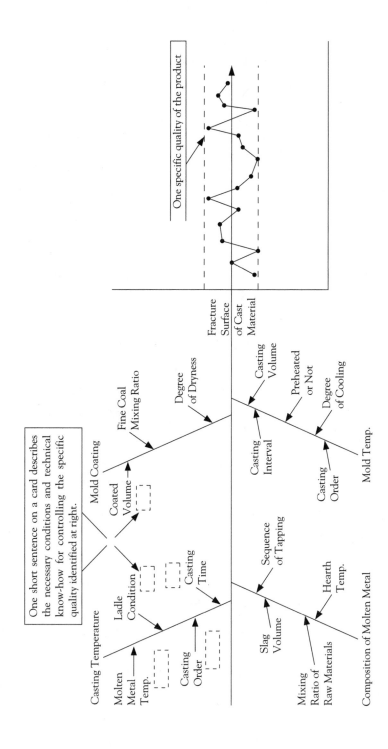

**Figure 10.3.** CEDAC. From *Management Engineering* by Ryuji Fukuda (used with permission).

*Step one.*   As a corporate body, describe the problem in detail to the assembled group, and allow participants to ask any questions that will better establish the limits of the problem. Allow no suggestions at this point.

*Step two.*   This is a round robin where the expression of ideas begins. The following ground rules must be stated and inflexibly enforced by the facilitator: Proceed around the circle person by person, allowing each to express only one thought per round. If a person cannot come up with an idea, he or she should pass. This does not eliminate participation on the next turn.

*Step three.*   At this point, no comments should be made by the facilitator or any member regarding the quality or appropriateness of any suggestion, and no suggestion will be thrown out or combined with another at this point. Humor and exaggeration are to be encouraged. A scribe will write out each suggestion on an easel pad to stimulate synergistic piggybacking of ideas.

*Step four.*   At the end of a set time, editing the discussion phase begins. Now misunderstandings are resolved and ideas better defined. Some of the ideas may be consolidated, if that's appropriate, and grouped.

*Step five.*   The facilitator asks members to vote on which ideas on the refined list will be useful in solving the problem and which will not. Members may vote for as many ideas as they desire.

*Step six.*   Ideas deemed unlikely to be useful should not be discarded. Some may be diamonds in the rough. In this consensus phase, each member of the brainstorming group votes for only one idea. The purpose here is to reduce the final menu to an acceptable scope.

*Step seven.*   Having harvested the best ideas and reduced them to a manageable menu, determine their relative merits. Which are practicable from a resource standpoint? Which are likely to produce the best results? Now assign responsibility for implementation—who will be in charge and who assists and supports. An essential element in brainstorming is to follow up with a plan of action derived by corporate effort. It is essential to establish that this is a serious undertaking and also to ensure that needed resources are made available.

## QUALITY CIRCLES

Quality circles can identify problems, verify the validity of a problem, gather data to support the contention, brainstorm the cause, collect supporting data, brainstorm the solution, verify its validity, and determine cost and value gained before presenting all this to management for approval and implementation. In addition, they offer a wide scope for employee action. Circles can address such issues as quality, efficiency, productivity, and cost reduction; they can work on topics like facility planning, tool design, production control, administrative procedures, image enhancement, and customer relations. In short, quality circles can solve problems.

Following are some of the goals quality circles will achieve when implemented. Benefits include:

- Raising the status of employees
- Exploiting workers' accumulated wisdom and creativity
- Helping individual development
- Unifying the group
- Achieving mutual education
- Recognizing workers' achievements
- Giving employees a sense of ownership
- Providing employees an incentive to do better

### Data Collection and Display

An important aspect of quality circles is the management presentation. (The term *management* as used here refers to whatever level has the authority to approve the proposal.) This is the time when the circle presents the solutions to the problem that either you or they have identified. At such a presentation, I suggest to management the three be's of success: be present, be responsive, and be appreciative. Otherwise, you may demotivate the group. Once the fact gets around that the boss really doesn't support quality circles, look out. You've just unleashed a bomb.

Here are two more suggestions for management. First, emphasize interest by providing resources, recognition, and reward to circles, and by participating. Second, don't expect instant acceptance of the circle concept—or instant results.

## SUGGESTION SYSTEMS

As a nation of independent free thinkers, some among us function better as individuals than as group members. Ideas from these people may require individual recognition, as well. For such people, a suggestion system is a natural.

Can a suggestion system coexist with quality circles? Yes. A suggestion system, when properly administered, is just one more effective method of harvesting ideas.

The key to success in a suggestion system is organization and administration. Your quality improvement process steering group is an ideal source for the ground rules. Establishing the rules gives the group ownership of the system, determines who is eligible, sets up the chain of command for evaluation and approval, and provides the tracking system necessary to make certain that suggestions are moving and duplication is avoided.

Of equal importance is determining the system of recognition and reward to stimulate participation. Avoid appealing to avarice and keep rewards modest. Recognition, though, should be highly visible. Big-money incentives can become a nightmare of legal and financial problems you never imagined, but merchandise, privilege, and modest cash prizes can generate enthusiasm and participation. Bear in mind that employees are already being paid for their efforts (wages/salary).

Sloppy or indifferent administration has killed many suggestion systems. Processing that takes six months to a year, rejection because of envy or threat to the status quo, failure to investigate poorly understood suggestions—all of these can cause suggestion systems to fall flat. The temptation to belittle suggestions is another thing that will completely kill a suggestion system. Evaluation of suggestions and notification to participants should take place within 30 days. An aggressively administered and publicized system, with visibility given to implementation, will effectively stimulate participation.

## STATISTICAL PROCESS CONTROL

Statistical process control (SPC) through use of control charts is a recognized approach to assuring control of manufacturing processes. In 1950, W. Edwards Deming presented this technique (developed by Walter A. Shewhart of Western Electric in the early 1920s) to Japan's top industrial management. He predicted that if they implemented process control, the world would beat a path to their door within five years. Prophetic words.

Can (SPC) assist you in reducing scrap, rework, and repair? Absolutely. Statistical process control, to some, smacks of a black art. Actually, it is only the application of data to monitor whether or not a manufacturing process is within acceptable limits.

We live in a world of variables. It's statistically impossible to achieve exact repeatability in any mechanical function. There are many unavoidable variables in any manufacturing process. We can live with a *degree* of variability. Thus, specs are written with a plus-or-minus tolerance.

Statistical process control says that, as long as we can set upper and lower critical limits that accommodate the tolerance specified, we can produce acceptable products. The smaller the variation between these limits, the better. By gathering, averaging, and plotting data during the production process, we can determine when we begin to exceed the limits and take corrective action. It may be that our measurements are askew or our machines need adjusting. Thus, we save the agony and cost of scrapping our material or investing time to rework or repair an item.

### Characteristics of Distribution Curves

*Control Charts* $\bar{X}$ and $R$ charts, sometimes called average and range charts, are statistical control charts and are illustrated in Figure 10.4. An $\bar{X}$ chart indicates the average of a scale of measurements, with $R$ indicating the range or difference between highest and lowest in a sample. $\bar{X}$ and $R$ charts give the operator an indication of when a process is both in and out of control. By checking first the data, then the process, the operator can take the necessary action to return to statistical control.

$P$ charts, another type of statistical control chart, require no measurements, only a count of the number of pieces that have like or unacceptable characteristics.

*Histograms and Pareto Analysis*   Histograms provide another visually meaningful way to plot data. For example, by plotting two desired variables, each of which possibly bears on the problem you are analyzing, on a bar graph, you achieve a visual representation of the dominant characteristic extant (Figure 10.5, top).

Vilfredo Pareto (1848–1923) was an Italian economist and sociologist remembered most for the analysis that bears his name. He suggested that, by grouping items of greatest quantity or importance on the left side of a bar graph and arranging items of lesser quantity or importance in descending order to the right, it is possible to make a rapid visual comparison of the data. A cumulative line can be added to demonstrate visually the value of each bar as an increment of the total (see Figure 10.5, bottom).

Pareto charts can be used to graphically display time, money, people, products, or other variables. By stratification, they can be used to determine where sheer numerical size is dominant, or whether other elements, such as total number of product defects by line, by shift, by process, or by value, more readily identify where effort will provide the most payback. Through use of Pareto analysis, hidden problems can be readily discerned.

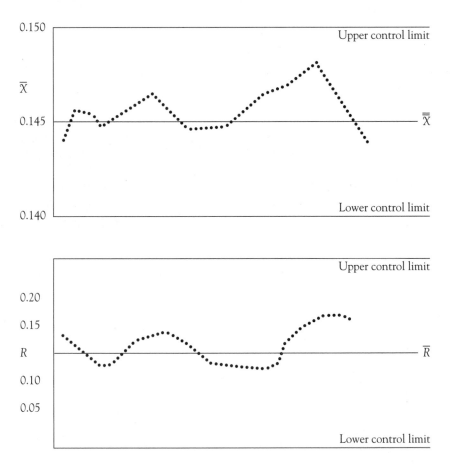

**Figure 10.4.** $\overline{X}$ and $R$ charts.

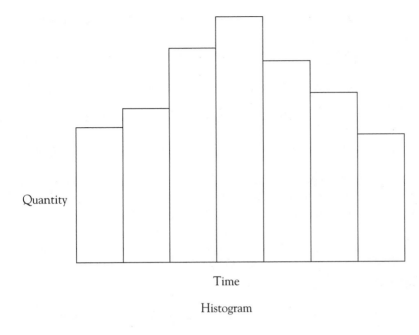

Quantity

Time

Histogram

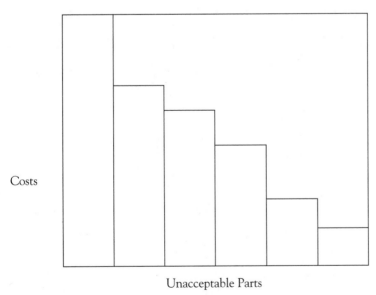

Costs

Unacceptable Parts

Relative Value of Unacceptable Parts

**Figure 10.5.** Pareto chart.

Joseph M. Juran made Pareto's 80/20 theory famous by labeling it "the vital few vs. the trivial many."[1] For example, in marketing, 20 percent of the sales personnel may account for over 80 percent of the sales, and in quality control, the bulk (80 percent) of the field failures, downtime, shop scrap, rework, sorting and other quality costs may be traceable to a vital few (20 percent) workers, machines, or processes.

## FLOWCHARTS

A flowchart is an analytical tool used to help determine the most logical path for a process in manufacturing or the sequence to take in unraveling a problem. It assists you in not only visualizing what needs to be done, but also helps you communicate that process to others. In essence, it is a pictorial representation of all the steps in a process, which helps the mind to more readily comprehend.

Flowcharting uses standard symbols to indicate the type of process being performed. Figure 10-6 gives an example of these symbols and of an application.

## VALUE ANALYSIS AND ENGINEERING

Lawrence Miles, father of value analysis and engineering, states, "The constant and accelerating flow of new ideas, new processes, new products, and new materials can, when properly applied, aid in establishing desired customer values at a lower cost. This leads to the conclusion that, when a product is designed, tooled, and on the market, it is already advancing to becoming obsolete."[2]

*Value* means a fair return on investment, and the customer defines *fair*. Value has nothing to do with being the most expensive of a kind. Value arises from worth being equal to or exceeding the price paid. Worth, in turn, may arise from an item's usefulness—its ability to perform a function to the customer's satisfaction.

Satisfaction depends on reliability. An automobile that starts 99 percent of the time is not considered by its owners to be reliable if it doesn't start when they have to take their injured child to the emergency room.

Another element of value is longevity. Is the warranty a prediction of the date of product failure? If so, the customer will interpret breakdown as part of the manufacturer's plan. If planned failure *is* part of the manufacturer's plan, then the manufacturer doesn't understand value.

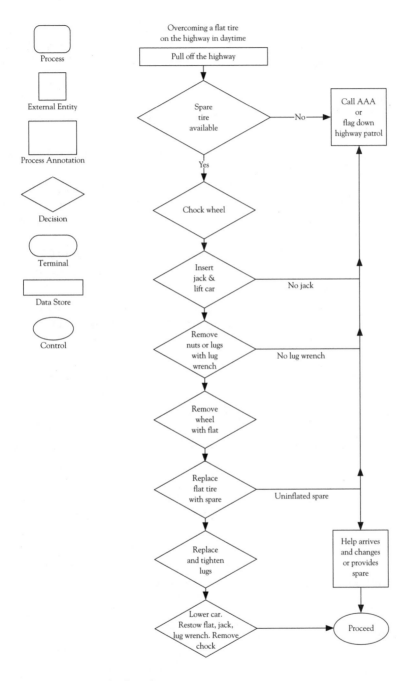

**Figure 10.6.** Sample flowchart.

*Value analysis* is particularly useful in determining how to achieve maximum value for a product or process. A logical first step in the value analysis process is to determine just who your customer is. Determine what you make or do for him or her (what satisfactions you provide) and determine whether you provide this service or product at the lowest possible price.

Bill Domings, the value analysis chief of the Paul Revere Insurance Companies, says that any process that has not undergone change in two years has probably fallen behind the power curve. Today's rapidly changing technology doesn't allow dormancy.[3]

Value can be increased by honestly questioning everything you do. Not only is it important that you do things the most efficient way, you must question whether you are doing the *right things*. Perhaps you're only doing what you'd like to do or what you're told to do.

Value analysis (VA), judiciously done, can produce substantial savings and improved quality. It takes time, however, and if management is not prepared to allow time for VA, expectations will never be fulfilled.

*Value engineering* is simply an organized approach to identifying consumer expectations while a product is in the concept and design phases. How can these be met at the lowest cost? There must be an exhaustive study of what the product is expected to do, how long it is expected to last, the degree of reliability expected, and the maximum competitive price. As price decreases with no corresponding decrease in function, reliability, or longevity, value increases. This collection of data requires input from quality, purchasing, design, manufacturing, and marketing. When it's time to act on the data—to begin moving the product to market—those groups must function as one team to meet the customers' expectations.

Value engineering looks not only at the functional technology of the product, but also at the materials that best fit the product, the tooling required, and the production and test sequences needed to bring this product to market on time and at expected cost. Value engineering questions every step of the design and development phases of new products, and basically uses the same sequences used in value analysis of a process.

## VERIFICATION

The final step in any approach to assuring quality is the verification phase. This is one of the first questions a top manager must ask when a quality circle or small group wants to make a managerial presentation: Has the validity of their problem been verified?

Elevating problem solving to an important position in the manufacturing, engineering, or purchasing department is one of the smartest single actions a manager can take.

## KEEPING YOUR FINGER ON THE PULSE

The eight problem-solving approaches discussed in this chapter are not new. They all carry the seed of success to the extent that management is involved. Support is not enough; participation is essential. Part of that participation requires keeping your finger on the program's pulse and being ready to act when the pulse gets weak, for none of these approaches will effectively run indefinitely on its own. Checks and fine tuning, or even radical changes, keep enthusiasm alive and efforts productive.

A change of leadership in the quality circle or small group activity from time to time will do wonders. Keep your eye cocked for wind shifts; otherwise, you may suddenly find your ship adrift or capsized. As the skipper, your responsibility is to see that this does not happen.

## NOTES

1. J. M. Juran, editor, *Quality Control Handbook*, 4th ed. (New York: McGraw-Hill, 1988), 2–16.

2. Lawrence D. Miles, *Techniques of Value Analysis and Engineering*, 2d ed. (New York: McGraw-Hill, 1972), 13.

3. Remarks by Bill Domings of the Paul Revere Insurance Companies at value analysis course to Textron, Inc., Leesburg, Va., July 7, 1986.

# 11

# TEN ESSENTIAL INGREDIENTS FOR ACHIEVING A QUALITY CULTURE

The quality discipline has long been beset by a mishmash of acronyms. Therefore, I would like to introduce a nonacronym that has not only meaning, but value in offering a viable solution to the problem of being successful in a very competitive international marketplace. That nonacronym is *quality culture*.

## QUO VADIS?

An effective commander plans a campaign with a goal in mind. In Desert Storm it was to rid Kuwait of Iraqi forces. Many, including I, thought this meant ridding Iraq of Saddam Hussein. However, General H. Norman Schwarzkopf's orders from the president and the United Nations Security Council said nothing about freeing Iraq of its leader.

So what is it that brings you to the point where you feel things need changing in your organization? Sales falling off, high turnover of personnel, customers dissatisfied with your product or service, a competitor now in your territory wooing your customers, overhead costs escalating, or perhaps just no growth? Any of these is a definite signal that spurs a successful leader to contemplate change.

The question is, what needs to change? Unfortunately, too often we latch on to the latest catchy acronym and decide to implement that without really understanding either *how* to do it or *what* it will do for you. What I suggest is that you begin with a change in the *basics* of your organization. Some may regard this as a philosophical discussion with little application to correcting their problem. Bear in mind that the how to's will be described in

131

chapters 12 and 13. Before we begin building the house, we must first lay the foundation. One of the greatest problems for America's industrial and business leaders has been neglecting to lay a solid foundation before beginning the superstructure. The 10 concepts that follow are essential for success in today's very competitive environment.

## TEN STEPS IN BUILDING A FOUNDATION FOR QUALITY

### Step 1: Basic Understanding of the Nature of a Quality Culture

What do we mean by a *quality culture*? This leads to definition of *culture*. One definition given by the *American Heritage Dictionary* is "the totality of socially transmitted behavior patterns, arts, beliefs, institutions, and all other products of human work and thought characteristic of a community or population." Boiled down, it's the sum of the beliefs, actions, and mores of a people. It's what people believe is *important* enough for them to accept and act upon. Add quality in the work culture and you have a group of people who believe that putting quality in their work makes the work itself important enough to *always* be done properly. There are two important concepts in this definition: first that their work—or what they do—is important. They put themselves in the role of the customer who is to receive that product or service, and they consider the standards by which the customer would judge their work or service. Second, their consideration of the product itself. Is it important? What function does it serve or contribute to the whole? For example, take the job of placing the wheels on or engine in an auto as it passes down the assembly line. Is the auto itself important? What function do the wheels or engine contribute to the completed automobile? Are there any totally unimportant parts? When people understand that what they do is important to society, to the economy of this nation then, and only then, will they understand the meaning of a quality culture and then, and only then, will the United States have achieved the sustainable competitive advantage necessary for long-range success.

### Step 2: Recognizing and Understanding the Dynamics of Cultural Transition

When I first suggested the concept of a cultural change to a group in Israel, their first reaction was: "Why would we want to change our culture? It is thousands of years old, much older than the culture of the United States."

After I explained that I was not interested in changing their ethnic culture, but rather their productive culture, they relaxed somewhat and then reacted a second time: "Who is going to do this *for* us?" Too often this is the attitude of managers who have suddenly learned that they must implement TQM in their organization. The first thought in their minds is "Who shall we get to implement TQM for us?" As a result, thousands of entrepreneurs have gone into the consulting business to implement TQM in American companies. If TQM is to be implemented to any degree, it will be done by the *organizations* themselves. Why? Simply because they are the only ones who really understand the business they are in, the constraints they must deal with, and the rewards—including staying in business—they can gain.

When I stated to the Israeli group that the change agents for this significant occurrence would come from their own ranks, they suddenly looked around in disbelief: "What, no consultant to come in and do this for us?"

"No," I said, "The selection of change agents to bring about a quality culture is nondelegatable. The only people who can change the culture are those who understand the nature of their culture and are willing to set an example in changing it. Until top people demonstrate the need for and the nature of the cultural change, few below them in the hierarchy will buy in to the concept."

What does the heading of this section mean by *dynamics* of the change? Simply that it is neither quick nor easy to change a culture. This may be the station at which many of you step off this train of progress I am describing. If you do, you will be missing one of the most exciting opportunities in your lifetime to see positive things happen. To those of you who elect to stay aboard, I congratulate you for your perseverance and courage.

### Step 3: The Nonexclusionary Nature of the Transition to a Quality Culture

The transition must be led by the major domo, the top banana, the honcho, or whatever pet name the CEO goes by. That person must be the chief agent of change. This is a trickle-down process where *follow-by-example* is the watchword. As the lower-pay echelons of your organization notice that management is really and truly committed to change, they will enlist with enthusiasm.

This must be a no-exception movement that begins at the top and becomes epidemic. If vice presidents, directors, managers, and line supervisors become involved in the process, the remainder of your organization will galvanize into becoming a part of it. The only complaint I have ever heard from an organization implementing this change was, "Management is not moving fast enough. What's the matter? Can't they see the advantage of what's happening?"

### Step 4: Up-Front Investment Required
"There is no such thing as a free lunch."

Believe it! Even the air we breath requires effort. The start-up and maintenance costs of changing the culture are high. But then consider the cost of nonconformance, the cost of lost customers, the competitor who is eating your lunch, as offshore competitors have done to our automobile and electronic industries. The difference between what a cultural change will do and what your competitors are doing is that the former gives you an opportunity to turn the tables and create a sustainable competitive advantage.

*Facilitator is required.*   The facilitator, whether internal or external, must understand the nature of changing a culture and the rock-hard mind sets that will be encountered. That person must also understand the value that the cultural change will bring to the organization and be able to translate that value into understandable terms for all strata of personnel. For top management, the terms are money, profit and loss, and the company's future. For middle management, they must be improved opportunity for advancement as the company grows and diversification of effort. On the production floor, the terms are continued employment, advancement, greater opportunity for education, and change in their own jobs. Once these groups understand the change in their own terms, you will have all of them excited about the future—their future with the company. Bonuses and benefits from increased competitive strength will be recruiting tools that few if any can resist.

The training and reorientation of thinking that go with the cultural change are the costly parts of the transition. But they must be weighed against the importance of success and survival. When one looks at the economic disarray of the 1990s in the United States, most spawned by poor, short-sighted and self-serving leadership in industry, business, and politics, it is easy to see that we cannot afford a repetition if the nation is to survive.

### Step 5: Long-Range Nature of the Concept
The old saying, "Rome wasn't built in a day," is applicable to this cultural change. Cultural change is not something that will happen in a quarter,

three quarters, or even a year. It is a long-term investment, for once you begin the movement, you will find that it requires continuing fuel to keep its momentum. This fuel is continuing follow-up, training, update of equipment, continuous research and development, and planning to see what your customers want and how you can best supply it.

For far too long, the United States has dealt in near-term profits and planning. When you have no competition, this is perhaps an acceptable way to manage. However, when hardball begins, beware: The goal is success and the means is winning the customer's loyalty. These are achieved only by perceiving what the customer wants and convincing each one that he or she is the most important part of your business. This aspect of management applies to both your internal and external customers.

By the time you have worked yourself to the top of the heap, your outlook may be somewhat short-range. However, consider the people on the line or out in the field. They may have just begun their careers and their goals are probably long-range. As the CEO of Xerox, David Kearns, said when he accepted the Baldrige Award, "Quality is a race with no finish line." As you get better, your competitor improves and the expectations of your customer increase, since technology continues to advance and mature.

### Step 6: Individual Ownership Essential for Success of Concept

What does *individual ownership of the concept* actually mean and is it really necessary?

Individual ownership means just that: Each person in your organization must look upon this cultural change as if it was his or her own idea and something of personal importance for the future. It must be something that employees believe will change their opportunity to grow in the organization and profit from their efforts and ownership. Why do people prefer to buy, rather than rent, their house? While renting provides an accumulation of rent receipts and a place to live and little else, ownership implies growth in equity of an investment. In work, the investment a person makes is their time. Does it amount to anything more than a paycheck? Or does their time investment become a part of the company's success, in which they will rightfully share?

This is one of the issues with which the facilitator must contend. He or she must recognize that the concept, once embraced by the individual, becomes a part of his or her fortune, his or her heritage. Failing to recognize this, little enthusiasm will be ignited in your associates.

**Step 7: Understanding the Complexity of the Concept**
There is nothing easy about this step.

It is complex because it involves *people*, and there is nothing simple about God's most complex creation. The body, legs, and arms are things we can deal with. But when God created men and women with minds and gave them the capability of independent thought, the concept of simplicity expired.

When I speak to a large group, I often wonder what they hear me say. From the looks on their faces, they're apparently intently grasping every word I am saying. Even their body language appears to confirm that they are accepting both the concept of changing a culture and their part in bringing about the change. Yet, until I ask a few pointed questions, I am not certain that they are even listening, much less absorbing the thoughts I offer. The concept, which to me seems so clear and easy to embrace, may be pure Greek to the people in the audience.

I contend that one of the strengths of the United States is diversity of opinion. Many contend that the homogeneity of the Japanese culture gives that country an advantage industrially. I believe that diversity of opinion causes people to question and search for reason and facts.

Am I contradicting what I said in Step 6? Not really. When I say that creating individual ownership in a cultural change is positive and desirable, I am suggesting that this be accomplished through the next step. Meanwhile, as you are considering the elements of your cultural change game plan, bear in mind that the subject of change to a complex individual may not initially accept your assurances that a cultural change is in his best interest. Don't underestimate people's intelligence and individual thought processes.

While the concept itself is not overly complex, the individual who must buy in is incredibly complex.

**Step 8: Being Alert and Prepared to Respond to the WIIFM**
The first thought that will flash in the mind of each of your employees will be, "Why should I?" The second will be, "What's in it for me [WIIFM]?"

Both of the questions are normal. The answer to the first one is obvious to those of us who have bought into the truth: If we want to maintain a competitive advantage as competition constantly increases, we *must* change. But bear in mind that many of your employees may *not* have reached that plateau of comprehension yet. I often wonder why Detroit took so long to identify the nature of the offshore competition and the disposition and proclivity of the customer. Is it because I am so much smarter than the top people in the

U.S. auto industry? Or were they so close to the problem and doing so well financially that they had not yet felt the personal sting of plant closings and layoffs?

The second question, WIIFM, is also perfectly natural. So you want me to change. What is in it for me? More money, an advancement, shorter working hours, more benefits? What did you have in mind, facilitator?

How would you, while extolling this important concept, answer this question? And don't forget, it can be articulated orally, by the furrowed brow, or by other equally obvious manifestations known as *body language*.

Continued employment might be the first response to pop into your mind. This is a very valid and very basic benefit of changing the culture to become more productive, more innovative, and more customer oriented. But before you begin to answer, have a number of WIIFMs ready to respond to your associates. The last thing you want to do is to reply, "Why, isn't it obvious what you will get out of it?" If it were obvious, they would not have asked the question. Or perhaps it is obvious to them and they are trying to see if *you* know what the benefits are.

Remember also that each level of employee has its own set of WIIFM motivators for this revolutionary cultural change you are describing. Get your list of "What's in it for me" in the proper order to appeal and apply to the group you are talking to.

**Step 9: Active, Effective Communication**
Perhaps the medium found consistently in greatest disarray in the American business, industrial, and political arenas, is effective and active communication within an organization. President Reagan and President Bush are positive and negative examples of efficacious communications. Result: two terms versus one!

In the early primaries of 1992, after the short and decisive Desert Storm campaign to drive Saddam Hussein out of Kuwait, President Bush awoke to find that all of the advantage that he had garnered from that war had suddenly vanished. He had not only a contender for the presidential nomination from his own party for the presidency, but the opposition party had suddenly taken heart and began posing a threat. The reason? Mr. Bush had not kept his ear to the ground to see what people were thinking and what was troubling them. The same thing has happened in many businesses: they have suddenly awakened to find that their internal as well as external constituents had deserted them for Brand X!

To be effective, communication, whether in the family or in an organization, must be two-way communication. We have to not only speak, but we have to listen and be sensitive to how the other party is responding to what *we* are saying.

Thus, when you undertake a complex project such as changing the culture of your organization, it is vitally important that you pay close attention to how employees are responding, what questions they are asking, whether their questions indicate genuine interest in what you are saying or out-of-hand rejection because of your past track record in their behalf. Your listening ability can be an important and powerful indicator of how far the cultural change concept is going to advance.

It is also important not to nonchalantly reject their objections or questions. These must be important to them, or they would not have voiced them. Be as deliberate and thoughtful as possible in responding to their questions or comments. Doing so will pay rich dividends in your recruiting efforts.

**Step 10: Stay the Course**
Do these three words sound familiar? They should, as they represent one of former President Reagan's admonitions to Americans regarding the necessity to keep the pressure on the former USSR. Americans stayed the course, and today we have the Confederation of Independent States, which vitally needs the United States and the free world's help to survive. Who would have ever thought it would happen in the twentieth century? And yet despite the fact that the struggle was long and costly, the mission of causing the world to recognize that Communism was a losing political concept paid off.

Many might say, yes, but at what cost? For those who ask that question, I would respond, remember friend, there are *no free lunches.*

Changing the culture of your organization will not take as long proving that communism is a failing concept, nor will it be as costly. But bear in mind, it is not an overnight transition, even in our instant-oriented society.

So there you have the 10 steps that will provide a firm foundation for survival and success in the waning years of the twentieth century and the early ones of the approaching twenty-first century.

Would you like your organization to be a survivor—or a casualty—when century twenty-one arrives?

It's up to you.

# 12 SO YOU WANT TO ESTABLISH A QUALITY IMPROVEMENT PROCESS?

How do you go about putting your organization on a quality course? The answer is not simple. It requires management involvement and the dedication of resources adequate to the task. It is an ongoing endeavor that involves people, and as stated earlier people are complex.

There are 20 items extremely important in structuring a quality improvement process (QIP). These steps must be examined and understood by a company's quality improvement process steering committee (a description of the composition and functions of which are described in Step 2) which will then have the responsibility for determining the sequence and intensity of implementation of the actions needed to change the culture of the organization. The steps that follow represent the rudiments of an action plan guaranteed to give you positive results.

## STEP 1: MANAGEMENT INVOLVEMENT

Management involvement is where the process begins. Management must be physically as well as intellectually involved. The head person, the chief executive officer, the president, or the chair of the board has to be firmly committed, dedicated, and involved in the entire process or the attempt to institute a quality improvement process will fail.

Employees have become very cautious of new corporate strategies. They've seen new strategies come and go. They've seen management lose interest when significant results do not immediately occur. Consequently, many employees are skeptical about embracing new programs. The best way to prove your sincerity is to involve yourself in the undertaking. Your staff and your employees will be the ones who implement the process, but *you* must keep your finger on the pulse, *you* must be visible during the implementation phase, and *you* must be the one to whom people are accountable for the success of this venture.


## STEP 2: QIP STEERING COMMITTEE

If you want to become involved, then your second step is to find a group of positive-thinking, interested personnel for your QIP steering committee. Who should belong? Certainly department or division vice presidents, at least one hourly employee, and a quality circle facilitator should be members of this group.

If you can persuade a union leader to join the effort, you have a definite advantage over organizations in which the union decides to remain aloof. To convince a union leader of the value of the QIP concept requires you to talk in terms of expected results: improved quality of work life, enhanced competitive standing for the company (ensuring the employee's tenure through improved market share), and improved opportunity for increased remuneration by virtue of increased profit.

While the membership of this committee might not be entirely voluntary, the majority of members should be volunteers. This will help ensure enthusiasm and stamina for the long-range process to follow.

### Charter

Having determined the membership of the steering committee, you should briefly describe the charter under which you expect the group to operate. The purpose of the charter is to determine which of the elements of a QIP plan—outlined in following pages—they feel are necessary to improve the performance of the company. A word of warning: Don't encourage them to bite off more than they can chew. Partial implementation will provide a worthwhile payback. Putting too much on their plate at one time will only invite disaster. However, the group should be encouraged to make a long-range plan that will eventually tackle all of the features in the QIP. Along with the decision on the initial project, a plan of action and milestones should be devised to indicate when and by whom the goals will be implemented. These will provide benchmarks for measurement.

The QIP steering committee should report directly to you, the top manager. It should be encouraged to meet monthly to hear reports from action officers responsible for implementing various tasks. The steering group's primary job, after it's hammered out an all-encompassing QIP, is to monitor the progress of the endeavor.

A key member of the steering committee is the quality circle facilitator, assuming, of course, that you plan to implement quality circles, perhaps the most important initial factor in assuring your employees that you're serious about a QIP. (More about circles in Step 11.)

## STEP 3: QUALITY POLICY

While companies have policies for sick leave, vacation, retirement, hiring, pay, and promotion, incredibly enough, few have a quality policy. What does a quality policy do? Very simply, it sets forth the standards and definition of what the company means by *quality*. In addition, it establishes accountability for delivery of a quality product or service.

The quality policy statement need not be long, but it must be clear, concise, and comprehensive—something that can be provided to every employee with a reasonable assurance that he or she will understand what it means. Some goals set forth in a quality policy might be:

- To provide customers with a product or service that meets or exceeds their expectations.

- To provide employees with a desirable work environment, competitive remuneration, and satisfying personal challenge.

- To provide stockholders with a competitive rate of return on investment and with an image of competence and long-term stability.

To achieve these goals, you will need a high level of dedication from all employees and suppliers. Everyone must resolve to perform all aspects of his or her tasks as completely and thoroughly as he or she knows how, and to seek to improve all aspects of the organization for everyone's mutual benefit. The president or general manager of the company or division should sign the policy statement. It should be printed in a form that can be tucked in a pocket for ready reference, so no one will have an excuse for not following it.

A policy poster might state, "Quality is doing the right thing, doing it the right way, doing it right the first time, and doing it on time." Those four elements leave little room for misunderstanding what is meant by a quality policy.

The quality policy is determined by the steering group and then given to you, the top person, for approval and signature. Give the group a few guidelines on what you'd like to have included, but let the committee write the policy.

## STEP 4: LONG-RANGE PLANNING

Perhaps one of the more crucial shortcomings of American industrial and business leaders is their lack of understanding of survival planning. Since CEO tenures are normally of a very limited duration, few seem to plan beyond their anticipated term. The fortunes of their companies 15 or 20 years in the future are of little concern since they won't be around to take either credit or blame. This absence of visionary planning is one of the weaknesses that the Japanese observe when an American business enters the Japanese market to establish its own niche. "Are you here for the long run, or are you just here to turn a fast profit and then move out and let the customers wonder who will support or improve your product?" they ask.

As a result of this short-range outlook, which considers only next quarter's or next year's financial standing, the planning for training, facilities, R&D, and tooling, so essential for the introduction of new products or services five, 10, or even 15 years hence, is neglected more often than not.

The question may arise, "How can we possibly anticipate technological or community needs 10 to 20 years in the future?" The answer is much more apparent today than it was when Jules Verne wrote *Twenty Thousand Leagues Under the Sea* or when Buck Rogers was performing unbelievable feats in the comic strip 50 years ago that we take completely for granted now. It's called visionary planning, and it requires imagination and judgment. But it will weigh heavily on the survival of your company. The leapfrog advances of technology mandate thinking ahead not a quarter, but at least a decade and laying the foundation for survival over that period. The brainstorming technique described in chapter 10 is an effective method for *crystal balling* the future. The players? Any of your staff who can break out of the bonds of the present and consider what the future portends. "The sky's the limit" must be the catch phrase for such a planning session.

An evaluation period must follow, at a respectable interval, these reaching-for-the-stars sessions in which each idea is evaluated in the light of developing technology, social and political change, availability of resources, and market orientation. Let's take water management as an example. As I write this chapter, southern California is being flooded by Pacific-generated storms. After a week of downpours, pundits have stated that the six-year drought continues unaltered. My question is how can this be? The answer is obvious enough. As long as we can get Colorado River water, tapping nature's local solution to this arid area of California is a nonproblem. The fact of the matter is that water management, as long as we can eke out existence, is given little thought. After all, solving the water management problem is neither glamorous nor apt to turn a quick profit. Additionally, it is a long-term and, in all probability, a most expensive problem. In the not too distant future, the lack of water will become a critical problem to the residents and industries in southern California. Some enterprising and visionary organization could win fame and fortune by addressing the problem of how to stockpile water against future needs.

The Civilian Conservation Corps (CCC) of FDR vintage is an example of long-range planning by the government. The CCC took young, unemployed men off the street and put them in barracks under pseudo-military discipline and employed them on long-range projects of clean-up, reforestation, and other similar undertakings. The Works Project Administration (WPA) was a like approach to long-range, and in many cases visionary, planning that focused on this country's infrastructure. Many of the bridges built in the 1930s under WPA aegis still stand. We need more visionary managers at the helm of not only government but business and industry if the United States is to survive economically and socially.

## STEP 5: RECRUITING, SCREENING, AND HIRING

The most important element in any QIP is people. Often, we hire without a great deal of thought or research into applicants' experience, background, or, particularly, their attitude.

Marv Runyon, past president of Nissan America in Smyrna, Tennessee, says that one of the most important criteria for hiring at Nissan is how the prospective employee feels about the company. To be hired, a person has to be motivated by more than the pay or more than a job. The criteria used in assessing the potential employee focus on determining whether the person really wants to become affiliated with Nissan because it is a premier auto and truck manufacturing company.

A useful recruiting and screening program should determine how qualified a person is for a job, and this can be discerned from recommendations and from experience. This screening is certainly an important phase in determining the value of the applicant to the company. Educational background, while important, should be secondary to the person's potential for becoming a contributing employee. A good balance between education, experience, and attitude will ensure that a person's potential is realized. Being too quick to employ usually ends up in additional recruiting and training costs. The degree to which a company can reduce turnover adds to its quality quotient.

## STEP 6: ORGANIZING FOR A QUALITY CULTURE

While organization will not necessarily give you quality, it should definitely be a part of your QIP. The idea that your quality department is solely responsible for quality is one of the first myths to quash. Quality is an all-hands effort, which, if supported and participated in by everyone from the top to the bottom, will result in a product or service that will consistently please the customer. My personal observation is that when the head of quality carries the title of vice president and reports directly to top management, he or she achieves equal influence and peer status with other vice presidents (engineering, purchasing, manufacturing, finance). However, when the head of quality is a director or manager—particularly if the position reports to manufacturing or engineering—he or she tends to be less influential and visible.

Functional integration first of quality, design, and manufacturing will assure a quick start-up and minimal engineering change orders after production has begun. A clear understanding of manufacturing capabilities by engineering will ensure that you have a makable product; and with quality making certain that the process is controlled, you'll find few rejects coming out at the end of the line.

Second, purchasing, engineering, and manufacturing vice presidents must also be functionally integrated. If purchasing's philosophy is dictated by low bid, manufacturing will often find itself trying to assemble junk. By the same token, if there isn't effective integration of engineering and purchasing, it will be impossible for purchasing to understand the requirements that must be met to achieve the design criteria.

A third area of functional integration must be among design, marketing, and manufacturing. If marketing sells a product that is beyond the state of the art (particularly if it's done within a time constraint that precludes a serious study and test period), you're faced with potential failure. Marketing should understand the capabilities of design and manufacturing before beginning to sell a product.

A fourth functional integration should be among human resources, engineering, and manufacturing. What kinds of people does the company need to meet the requirements of the business you're in? What types of engineers do you need? What kind of experience should they have? What kind of production people are essential to run the plant properly? All of these questions must be answered by your human resource people, since they do the recruiting and hiring.

A fifth integration should be among administration, finance, public affairs, and management. What kind of image is desired for the company, low profile or high profile? Top management must make the decision on this and assure that the image is well understood within advertising, finance, and public affairs.

## STEP 7: TIME MANAGEMENT

What does the phrase, "I don't have time," really mean when offered as a response from a subordinate, or a superior? What do *you* mean by it when you offer it as an excuse for not doing something someone asks you to do?

How much time do you have to invest in all of your activities? If you said 168 hours per week, you are on target. And since this is *all* the time you will ever have, when you say "I don't have time" what you are actually saying is, "I don't want to do that," or "That is not on my priority list of things to accomplish." As my son-in-law LCDR Richard Silveira, CHC USNR has often said, "We do what we *want* to do." We use the excuse that we don't have time as an escape hatch for ducking the onerous, distasteful, or unfamiliar. The next time someone invites you to participate in something that interferes with what you are doing —be fair—state why you don't want to do it, but avoid the cliché of "I don't have time."

The question of time management is *not* how much of this precious unrecyclable time we have, but rather *what it is that we do* with this commodity.

Have you ever audited how you spend your day? Do it for a week if you want to know how productive you are. A waste of time, you say. Not really. Set up a format dividing your day into five or 15-minute segments. Then assign a letter of the alphabet to each of the productive things you should be doing and to the nonproductive things (coffee breaks, interruptions, daydreaming, calls to your spouse and friends). Finally at the end of the week, analyze how you have spent your week. You will suddenly find a block of precious time you didn't realize you had. Incidentally, make certain that you reserve a letter for planning—you may be surprised how little planning you do to effectively use your limited purse of time.

Sir Joshua Reynolds wrote, "There is no expedient to which man will not resort in order to avoid the real labor of thinking." Can you relate to that? I certainly can!

Effective time management is another important element of quality management. Knowing how much time to invest in various activities will go a long way toward your success and toward the sustainable competitive advantage of your organization.

A good investment of top management's time is seeing what is going on in the business. Doing so will help keep the company viable and competitive. Careful now—did I hear you say, "I don't have time?" Does that mean you dread being asked a question you can't answer—or worse—does that mean you are not prepared to *ask questions* that will make you more knowledgeable? Asking questions is one of the best ways to improve two valuable skills in your management effectiveness. First, you learn something about your business— don't be shy about knowing the business you are in and the details about it. Second, you would be surprised how much respect you will gain from employees and associates when you ask them what they are doing and they have an opportunity to tell you. This is a value-added move that shows you have an interest in your people. They may well conclude that you know the answer to the question you ask and are checking to see if *they* know what they are doing.

### Saving Time

Is it possible to save time? The answer is a flat *No!* As the World War II song goes, "Time waits for no one, it passes you by." Once that minute, half hour, or hour has raced by, it is gone forever. The only recourse you have is to brood later about how you could have wasted so much time, and ask yourself, "Where did the time go?" While time cannot be saved, it *can be used better*, and thus made more valuable. There are a myriad of ways to accomplish this. For example, get to work early and plan your day, or plan tomorrow before you leave the office today. When you don't want to be disturbed, so you can either meet a deadline or accomplish some creative work, tell your secretary that you want absolutely no interruptions. Finally, if you want real privacy, go off site, perhaps stay home. Just make certain that you accomplish something in the time you couldn't be reached.

Resist the urge to have a cellular phone in your auto. Transit time offers an excellent chance to think and record your thoughts, or to listen to tapes of important books or news significant to your business.

In your office, arrange your desk so that your back is to the door. You will not be distracted by everyone who drops in to say hello, and you can lend credence to your desire not to be disturbed by ignoring whoever is behind you.

When a visitor does encroach, stand up and stay standing as you transact business. By not asking your interrupter to sit down, you have insured yourself against a long visit. Use your airline trips by taking either a briefcase of work or accumulated reading material with you for both the long flights and the interminable waits in the airport.

## STEP 8: SUPPLIER CONTROL PROGRAM

Since most large companies now are assemblers or integrators, it's essential that the parts assembled, even if they are from subcontractors that furnish parts, meet the specifications of the ultimate customer. When you're considering buying parts from a supplier, make a thorough quality audit of its facilities, procedures, and systems so you will be sure the product you receive is one that will be on time and to specification.

If the supplier has a good quality assurance process, you should consider supplier certification, which allows you to accept the product as a result of receiving inspection sampling or even without inspection. If the supplier has no quality assurance system, you should, at least initially, do a source inspection or a near 100 percent receiving inspection. The source inspection, while a little more costly, can provide certain benefits. It avoids delay in incoming shipping time before you find out which parts are unusable. If there is an effective assurance system, an occasional spot check is generally adequate to ensure acceptability of the parts. In the final analysis, the supplier must be encouraged to institute an effective quality assurance system.

A supplier rating system is often desirable to show suppliers how they rate against your company's quality standards. It is always beneficial to have supplier briefings *before* the supplier begins furnishing a part. The briefing helps the supplier understand both the end product for which the supplier is furnishing a component and the operating conditions to which the product will be subjected.

I recall an incident where a supplier was producing blades for a high-speed gas turbine. The supplier's machine operators, all of whom were very dedicated workers, had no idea of the speed and temperatures these blades would encounter. Therefore, they failed to recognize the fact that tolerances had to be precise. The prime contractor began a program of orientation flights in the aircraft using these turbine blades. The prime contractor and the blade supplier quickly learned their lesson when they recognized that their lives depended on their work!

Annual briefings for suppliers, calling them all together to reiterate the quality desired and reveal any changes that might have occurred in the end product, are another excellent way to ensure good communication and good relations.

In addition to supplier briefings, a supplier recognition system works well to stimulate supplier excellence. Consider an annual contest to determine who is the best supplier. Make certain that it's based on performance and that it gets the proper publicity. Anything that causes suppliers to feel membership on your team is definitely to your advantage, and any methods that can be used to engender such identification are certainly worthwhile.

## STEP 9: INVENTORY CONTROL

Inventory represents money. It represents capital in the value of material or components tied up in inventory, and it represents money in the space needed to store it. Inventory also requires money for the people who are doing the handling. In general, the smaller an inventory you can carry, the greater will be your profit, and the more efficient your operation.

Naturally, the inventory must be the kind that can be used to support the production schedule. This entails good planning, which falls in the hands of your information specialist, or whoever is responsible for your materials requirement plan (MRP). It also depends a great deal on the suppliers of this inventory.

Inventory control and good MRP require a close liaison between your MRP manager, manufacturing, and purchasing. As long as you have functional integration of these people, there should be no question about the effectiveness of your inventory system.

## STEP 10: ACCOUNTABILITY

As in any useful system, it's absolutely essential that there be accountability for the process. This means that people must be assigned to implement each step. They must have an infrastructure that allows them to appropriately control the process, and, with that in place, they can be held accountable for actions. The QIP steering committee, of course, must make it understood that action officers will be accountable for seeing that the QIP program moves in the right direction. When problems must be encountered, they must be reported at an appropriate level for review and correction. Without accountability, little can be realized from any QIP.

## STEP 11: QUALITY CIRCLES

As stated earlier, quality circles can be one of the most vital elements of a QIP. They involve participative management in its most effective form.

Shop around for a good program and make certain that the person or firm who will do the briefing and subsequent training understands quality circles and displays competence. QCI International, located in Red Bluff, California, offers one of the soundest available plans for implementing quality circles.

After briefing your steering group, if you and the group agree on the value of quality circles, your next step is to choose facilitators. The facilitators should be people who feel at ease before a group and can effectively communicate. They should have the respect of their peers and be enthusiastic about quality circles. Otherwise, your quality circles may never get off the ground.

The facilitator is the person who trains the quality circle leaders and monitors them as they go through the training process with their circle members. After training is completed, the facilitator will be the person who occasionally sits in on the quality circles to monitor progress and serves as a back-up for circle leaders. (Facilitators also try to field questions for which leaders don't have sound answers.)

In small organizations, there should be at least one facilitator for every 50 people. Regardless of whether or not you're going to implement quality circles incrementally, this number represents a good facilitator-to-circle ratio. In larger organizations (500 to 10,000 employees), one facilitator can serve up to eight circles.

Once the scope of the quality circles has been agreed on, the number of facilitators and the amount of training material necessary can be determined. Circle size should be not smaller than three people and no larger than 15. Eight to 12 is an ideal size.

The facilitators have full-time jobs with the company and perform circle service only as a part-time effort. Part-time facilitators are recommended because they can continue their primary duties and thus maintain a more balanced profile. The facilitators will report to the steering group and will be a part of the deliberations on the QIP.

The facilitator normally receives three to five days of training that provides an understanding of group dynamics and engineered problem solving. After the training, the facilitator's responsibility is to train each of the quality circle leaders in the duties and techniques for interaction with members of the circles. If facilitators are trained offsite by an independent organization, training material is furnished. However, if training is done in-house, then materials similar to those used to train the leaders should be procured. Leader training is normally a day shorter than facilitator training. Before a facilitator is trained, the steering group should have made some decisions about the scope of the company's quality circles.

While most experts on quality circles indicate that circle membership should be voluntary, there are pros and cons to voluntary and mandatory participation.

Voluntary participation allows everyone to make up his or her own mind, and thus, they'll be better suited to operate in the quality circle environment. If participation is mandatory, everyone is introduced to the concept, making for a nonexclusionary type of atmosphere. In addition, this method generates the feeling that, if quality circles are good for one group of people, they should be good for all. This argument seems logical.

After both facilitators and leaders are trained, the normal procedure is to have an information meeting for implementation. It will outline the purpose of quality circles, the training members will receive, and the benefits to members and to the company. If membership is to be voluntary, people should be allowed, after some thought, to indicate whether they wish to join a circle. If it is going to be mandatory, then the information meeting serves to get employees familiar with the concept.

While facilitator and leader training usually takes a number of consecutive days, training for circles themselves normally requires a one-hour lesson each week for six to eight weeks, depending on the circle training desired. QCI International has an eight-meeting training course that ranges from an information overview of problem solving and problem prevention to pointers on management presentation.

As soon as leaders are trained, implementation of the quality circles concept should begin. The training generates tremendous interest and enthusiasm in leaders, and the sooner you can take advantage of that momentum, the better off you are.

The facilitator's function, after having completed training of leaders, is one of an overseer and a mentor. He or she becomes your command sensor to determine how well quality circles are doing and when it will be necessary to assist the leaders in directing or in revitalizing the circles. Usually, however, when the facilitator attends a meeting, he or she should be only an observer, responding only when invited to do so by the leaders.

## STEP 12: RECOGNITION SYSTEM

There are many different ways of recognizing the accomplishments of employees. Many managers feel that pay is the primary recognition, and some employers feel that it's the only one necessary. While salary scales are a basic means of recognition, people like personal acknowledgment from the boss. This can take the form of a pat on the back, a kind word from a manager walking around the plant, letters from top management, quality designations on the person's jacket or working garb, or publicity that gives plantwide recognition. All of these cost little, but can be effective in establishing a quality culture among your people.

Social functions, too—picnics, potlucks, or company dinners—can provide effective recognition of people who make outstanding contributions to quality, productivity, or other important functions.

Some companies believe that cash prizes or gifts that stimulate people to greater accomplishments. Many times an agreement with a local merchant for gift certificates can have a positive effect on employees' enthusiasm for the quality process.

Another type of award recognizes the quality team as a *whole*, with some monetary reward based on savings accrued as a result of suggestions implemented. This can be in the form of individual cash awards to each member of the circle or one cash award for the entire group, which can be used for a celebration, athletic equipment, or anything that the circle can enjoy collectively.

The choice of recognition is up to you. There should be distinct levels of recognition for various achievements, but a recognition program is definitely one that will earn dividends for the quality culture.

## STEP 13: SUGGESTION SYSTEMS

Many people are fulfilled by being a part of a successful team, but some prefer individual contribution and recognition. They feel quite capable of developing a suggestion completely by themselves and submitting it to management. And they, in turn, would like to get full credit for it. While the synergistic effect of quality circles cannot be disputed, neither can it be denied that some people are not team players and would prefer to make an individual contribution to the improvement of quality. By having a suggestion system as well as quality teams or circles, you can harvest all the ideas that employees have had for years but that have just never surfaced.

A word of warning, though. Don't start a suggestion system unless you're serious about going through with it. The possibility of a six-, eight-, or twelve-month lag between the time an idea is proposed and the time feedback is given is one that will kill a suggestion system.

Timely feedback requires an organization to review the suggestions and refer them to experts (industrial or design engineers, for example). They will determine if a suggestion is feasible and how much it will benefit the company when effected. There must be a feedback system that responds to the individual within two weeks, even if it's nothing more than an interim reply or an acknowledgment that the suggestion is now in the system. Take no more than six weeks to complete the review and inform the idea submitter of the results, so he or she understands that it is not languishing in someone's too-hard basket.

How do you reward useful suggestions? There are as many different ways of rewarding good suggestions as there are people who have them. One is to give the originator a percentage of first-year savings.

A caution regarding suggestion systems is that one must consider legal ramifications. Make certain you don't set yourself up for a lawsuit for having disregarded a suggestion or used one without any compensation. Have your legal department study this, and make certain that your suggestion system is well protected.

The key to any successful suggestion system, though, is to be responsive and fair to those who offer input. There is a great deal to be gained from such systems, and having quality circles in no way diminishes the power of this additional harvesting tool.

## STEP 14: CUSTOMER CONCERN

The reason service or manufacturing industries exist is, of course, the customer. Often this aspect of business somewhat fades from view as the customer becomes an impersonal name on an order form instead of a real identity whose success depends on how well a product or service fulfills the customer's expectations. It is therefore essential that a customer barometer measure exactly how the customer—whether a prime contractor or an end user—feels about the product. In either case, it's positive perception of the supplier's performance that ensures continued prosperity.

One thing to remember is that every organization has two distinct sets of customers. The better known group, the external customers, are those who purchase the final product or service (or a component if the organization does not supply to the ultimate user). This group is certainly important to the business, since it furnishes the revenue essential to remain solvent.

However, there is a second category of customer that most people overlook. These are the internal customers who make the product or provide the service. Are they as important as the external customer? Without question, since they too are the people responsible for the company's being in business. They *make* the product or *render* the service that makes it possible to have external customers. And yet, how seldom we treat these internal customers as being vital to the business. We often take them for granted, believing that they require nothing other than a paycheck. There may have been a time when wages were adequate to gain a worker's loyalty. Those days are behind us. Now internal customers require recognition and respect, as do our external customers.

There's actually a third customer group. This one consists of your suppliers. These customers are also extremely important since they supply either raw material or components for your product or service. If you are imprecise in specifying your needs to your supplier, you'll likely have difficulty satisfying the customer group that buys your product or service. Late deliveries from a supplier have a negative effect on your business, and often cause you to lose face, or worse, to your customers. What sort of quality culture does your supplier customer have? Is it sufficient for you to accept the supplier's material on a dock-to-stock basis, or must everything be inspected before it's either installed or put on the shelf?

How do we implement a customer satisfaction barometer? One way is through use of questionnaires. These should be designed to be easily completed by customers. In addition, they should make customers feel that you value both their business and their opinions about your product or service.

A simpler way to sample customer opinion is through a phone survey, which puts you in direct contact with customers and allows them to comment candidly on the product without a great deal of personal effort. This may not seem as comprehensive as a questionnaire, but certainly it has the potential to be much more candid. It is, however, an effective method.

A third approach to determining how customers feel about your product or service is personal contact—having your marketing or engineering people sit down with customers to get their opinions about what you're offering.

Still another tool is a feedback card accompanying each product or lot delivered. This works particularly well if postage is prepaid. Then the customer simply makes a few check marks and writes a few lines before dropping the card in the mail. With limited customer effort, you receive valuable information about your product or service.

## STEP 15: TRAINING PROGRAM

A well-organized, formal, documented training program is important to the success of your QIP. The assumption that qualified new hires need little training can lead to headaches later. A good orientation course and an observation period for new employees are essential to their long-term success. Welders, solderers, and critical assemblers should be certified and periodically requalified to assure competency.

Responsibility for developing the training should be formally assigned, and training accomplishments should be documented. The training program should have its own budget, controlled by top management. Otherwise, when the economy falters, the first budget to be cut will usually be training. If the training program is controlled by someone from top management, such cuts hopefully will be avoided.

Training can be accomplished either in-house or through outside consultants. If an outside consultant is used, investigate his or her qualifications thoroughly, and bear in mind that outside trainers do not understand your organization's needs as well as an in-house trainer. But in-house trainers must be as well qualified as outside consultants to ensure that your product will meet your customers' expectations.

## STEP 16: DESIGN INTEGRATION

Computer-aided design (CAD) has revolutionized product design. Creating a design that satisfies the customer's requirements is made easier by the ubiquitous computer, which we now generally take for granted because most cannot remember when we did not have this electronic aid. Disappeared are the old standbys—the slide rule, drafting table, and drawing instruments. Gone is the green eyeshade design engineer who labored far into the night to meet a design schedule.

The computer eliminates many tedious and time-consuming efforts of both manufacturing and design engineering. But the question remains, once we have designed it, can we manufacture it? I don't mean you should do a prototype in a well-equipped engineering lab with skilled technicians. That's often easy enough. The question remains can it be manufactured out on the floor with a group of people whose skills range from excellent to barely adequate? Will the installed machinery hold the tolerances required? Close coordination between production and engineering is an absolute must at this point in development. It is of little value to be able to design and build a prototype if you are unable to carry through the manufacturing phase.

### The Customers—Are They Included?

Another important factor in the design integration phase is the customer. How much liaison do you conduct during this phase? You have carefully gone over the specs and you honestly believe that you know the requirements. However, are you certain the *customers* know what they want? Many times customers have a fairly good idea of what they want, but once they see how you plan to execute the specs, a sudden change occurs between specs and expectations. One of the reasons the DOD has been plagued with cost overruns is because of the differences between original specifications and later expectations.

When I visited the Toshiba plant in Fuchu with a group of Avco Corporation executives, I posed these questions to the general manager: "How do you make certain that, before you cut chips, you are going to satisfy the expectations of your customer? Is it possible to provide what the customer wants without a great number of either price raising change orders or cost escalators that lower your income on a fixed price contract?"

Slowly, Yuzo Kojima, the general manager, answered. "Yes, it is possible to satisfy the customer, but only if you are willing to exercise patience and work very closely with customer representatives during the development phase."

"And how is this accomplished?" I asked, knowing this would ensure the rapt attention of my colleagues.

"When we get the specifications, we study them closely and determine what, in our mind, the customer is asking us to create. We then arrange a meeting with the customer and share our perceptions with customer personnel. 'No,' they might say, 'that is not exactly what we had in mind. Thank you for helping us clarify this misunderstanding. Here is what we actually desired.'

"So, back to the drawing board we go to execute some engineering concepts that include the customer-requested changes. Upon completion, we get together with the customer once more and ask, 'Is *this* what you had in mind?' During this meeting, customer representatives may agree that we now are on the same frequency, or again having new ideas, may suggest some changes. You may think, this is taking too long and wonder how we ever get to the prototype phase. The answer is simple. We begin the prototype when we *know* what the customer really wants and when we *are satisfied that the customer also knows*. After all, *the customer* is our reason for being in business.

"We follow this routine again during the building of the prototype. While this is a significant investment in up-front planning time, it pays great dividends when we begin cutting chips. Oh yes, it is important that my production engineers be in on this planning phase to get their concurrence on being able to build to the customer's expectations."

Being able to design to the customer's specifications is one thing; being able to build without a great number of changes with attendant production delays and additional cost is quite another. The planning time investment we put into a new product is like money in the bank.

## STEP 17: PROCESS CONTROL—A SYSTEMS APPROACH

### Process Capability
Of prime importance is *knowing* the capabilities of your manufacturing process or, put another way, the measured, built-in reproducibility of the product turned out by the process. Understanding if specification tolerances can be achieved, what production rates the process will support, and what maintenance requirements are necessary to hold tolerances, these are process capabilities that must be statistically derived.

There can be no question about process control's superiority to end-item inspection. The latter separates the good from the bad—it is hoped—and ensures that the product will be to the customer's liking. However, it does not help reduce the cost of nonconformance, which is generated through scrap, rework, repair, warranty costs, and customer dissatisfaction. Statistical process control, when applied to all vital dimensions, will assure that operators understand when a process is going out of control and at what point future parts will have to be reworked or scrapped.

Before a statistical process control procedure is initiated in the plant, explain its purpose to the operators. When the use of control charts is mandated without any explanation or training, you'll find a tremendous amount of resistance, and the installation of the process will be lengthy and costly. Controlling the process from concept to delivery is an important aspect of any QIP.

**Computer Software**

The introduction of computers into industrial use in 1978 provided an entirely new dimension to quality. While CNC equipment has expanded man's capability to replicate processes with greater accuracy, no CNC machine is better than the software that controls it. Some feel that the computer has made people somewhat obsolete in the quality equation, but bear in mind that it is the men and women writing and debugging the programs who are ultimately responsible for this magic. A program is no better than the programmer's understanding of the process—whether it be drilling, machining, grinding, polishing, plating, hardening, tempering, or extruding—and the machine by which it is to be accomplished.

Just as it can produce spec-perfect parts, a computer program can just as easily produce defective parts if poorly executed. All depends on the quality of the software and its implementation and maintenance. What steps have *you* taken to provide your software development and maintenance personnel with a quality improvement process?

## STEP 18: THE UNAFFORDABLE COST OF NONCONFORMANCE

Comedian Bob Burns, the bazooka humorist, used to feature a skit in which he explained why the leak in the roof never got fixed: "When it's raining, can't; when it ain't, don't need to." Failure to document the cost of nonconformance will predict, in much the same manner, continued nonconformance costs and all they imply about your earnings, the reputation of your product, and the morale of your personnel.

The value of determining the cost of nonconformance is indisputable. It makes the difference between a business with sustained market competitiveness and one that will limp along and eventually fail. Being able to identify where your profit drain will occur as a result of scrap, rework, repair, warranty costs, lost contracts, and legal suits is very important in structuring a program to stop this outflow of profit.

One method of beginning this cost collection process is by brainstorming the possible sources of nonconformance (this can be an activity for your QIP steering committee), one can then determine areas worth documenting. Once this is done, the scope of such a cost can be determined.

Nonconformance costs manifest themselves in design changes that cause production modifications, scrap, rework, and repair. Excess inventory to meet production schedules is another dimension of nonconformance costs. Contract delivery delays can result in penalties, loss of credibility, or contract cancellation. Post-manufacturing costs should likewise not be omitted from nonconformance calculations. These include field service reps, warranties, repair and replacement costs, and, most costly of all, loss of your firm's reputation and repeat business.

Consider just the cost of rework. In cost of labor alone, it represents three times the investment of doing it right the first time: first-time-through cost, rework cost (which will often be greater than the original cost), and the cost of not producing an additional item in the time being used for rework. Consider also the morale of your rework line. Are these individuals happy redoing work they or their associates have messed up?

Without a clear and concise method of documenting your cost of nonconformance, you will never know the magnitude of lost earnings or the sources of the costs. These costs should be calculated as a percentage of direct labor costs.

The cost of nonconformance, when properly calculated, will always get top management's attention, since money is a language that group understands. It also will gain the attention of workers who can recognize their loss of competitiveness in the marketplace. In companies with a profit-sharing plan, advertising the cost of nonconformance can be an *exceedingly* effective way to gain the attention of the workers.

Defects are not free. Industry calculations indicate that nonconformance costs run from 10–40 percent of direct labor costs. Once sources are identified and a corrective action program developed, a monitoring procedure can determine the efficacy of the corrective action system and ensure a trend going in the right direction. It's important that the trend be charted so all employees will be able to understand the value of their efforts in the improvement of productivity.

Achievement of a quality culture is entirely possible, but only to the extent you know the nature and roots of your quality problems.

## STEP 19: AUDIT

So how do you implement process control if you no longer depend on 100 percent inspection? Note that I *did not* say eliminate first-article inspection. This remains essential to determine whether your process, as designed, is capable of meeting the customer's desires, needs, and expectations. We have already learned to our dismay that, as a result of increased offshore competition, wholesale end-item inspection is not only too costly, but is not 100 percent effective in ensuring quality. The cost of nonconformance, which manifests itself in scrap, repair, rework, warranty, and lost customers, is a surtax we cannot afford if we intend to compete. It is essential then that we reorient our thinking about how to achieve the degree of perfection necessary to succeed.

The answer is audit.

The audit begins in the derivation of new concepts, and proceeds throughout design, engineering, purchasing, production, marketing, and servicing our product or service. The audit philosophy holds each associate responsible for his work. Quality personnel disappear from the scene as police and reappear in the role of auditor to ensure that the system is functioning as designed. In the Nissan plant I visited in Oppama, Japan, each person was responsible not only for his or her own quality performance, but also for checking the quality of the preceding procedure. It works. Auditing reduces costs and increases the effectiveness of your quality management process.

## STEP 20: BENCHMARKING

You have accepted the challenge to become more competitive. You are not satisfied to be run over by the competition. You have faith that your product or service, your associates, and your marketing approach can compete with anyone. Now you want the answer to the question, how good must you be in order to stay ahead of the competition?

First of all, never compare your company with organizations doing more poorly. You don't need lessons in failure. What you need to learn is what the winners are doing—like Xerox, Motorola, Globe Metallurgical, Westinghouse Commercial Nuclear Fuel Division, Milliken Mills, Federal Express, Cadillac, Wallace, or IBM Rochester to name some of the Baldrige Award winners. These are organizations that have established world-class standards of operations.

You can learn how they achieved the level of excellence that brought them international recognition. One of the advantages that the Baldrige Award offers American business and industry is that the winners must share the secrets of their success. But you need not go to that length; just look around at organizations not only in your industry or product line, but at others doing well. Observe how they treat their customers, both internal and external, and their suppliers. Notice how they market. Learn how much they spend on research and development. Find out how they measure customer satisfaction. Determine the financial controls they use to ensure their overhead is acceptably low, allowing them to make a profit and successfully compete.

Always choose companies more successful than your own to emulate and to learn from. Don't be afraid to adopt others' ideas, but modify them to suit your organization. Consider this: On the tomb of Andrew Carnegie is the inscription, "Here lies a man who was not afraid to hire a man smarter than himself." You might paraphrase this for your own use by saying, "Mine is a company unafraid of borrowing and using ideas that bring success, regardless of where they originated."

Self-satisfaction can sound the death knell to any business striving to succeed.

Go for it.


## SUMMARY

What should be apparent after you've read through the 20 steps involved in setting up a quality improvement process is that a successful QIP focuses on three essential elements of quality.

The first is *quality of management*. As I said at the beginning of this chapter, unless the top person is interested in more than survival, is interested instead in achieving a sustained competitive market advantage, talk of a QIP is futile. Deming and Juran agree that the majority of errors negatively affecting quality and productivity can be laid at management's door; therefore, let's concentrate first on straightening out that aspect.

Chapter 9 is devoted to the second essential element of a QIP, *quality of (work) life*. A program to enhance the quality of work life looks at hiring the appropriate people, giving them necessary training to develop a confident and proper attitude, providing them with adequate tools to do a first-rate job and facilities that give them reason to have pride in and identity with the company, and then supporting them with the kind of recognition that says, "*you are* our most important asset and we appreciate your best efforts."

The third element is *quality of performance.* This is where customers become aware of just how important (or unimportant) the company believes they are to its sustained competitive market advantage.

These three elements are covered thoroughly in the 20 steps I have outlined. May you have great success in applying them.

**Author's note:** The 20 steps in establishing a quality improvement process are used with permission of Quality Printing and Graphics International, Inc., publisher of *Twenty Steps in Building a Quality Culture,* © 1986.

# LEADERSHIP:
# 13 THE MISSING
# FOUNDATION

The theme for the Ninth International Conference on Quality Assurance hosted in 1992 in Jerusalem by the Israel Society for Quality Assurance was "Quality—The Bridge to Harmony and Prosperity." This is an appropriate subject in a world beset with so many problems involving international competition for markets and at the same time trying to meet the demands of nations emerging from totalitarian government economic control with the attendant dearth of consumer goods.

Certainly quality *is* the bridge to harmony (read *peace*) and prosperity, two ingredients that are lacking in our civilization today. The Middle East in particular has been the locale for much disharmony, as demonstrated by the aggressive acts of Iraq, Iran, and Syria—in some cases territorial aggression, in others support and export of terrorism. Has this been an obstacle to these countries in their quest for prosperity? Without question it has been. National resources spent in waging war or training terrorists robs society of the challenge to progress, grow, and create a more fulfilling opportunity for people everywhere.

## DOCUMENTATION AND TECHNOLOGICAL ADVANCES ADEQUATE FOR NOW

Documentation-wise we are surfeited. For decades MIL-Q-9858A, MIL-I-45208A and Standard Form 32 were considered adequate, if not completely understood. Now ISO 9000 puts forth a quality assurance management system that goes into great detail producing what British Standards Institution (BSi) terms a "systematic framework for the consistent application of common

163

sense." Metrology-wise, the quality discipline has progressed significantly. Our ability to measure, inspect, and do failure analysis is impressive. The silicon chip and computer have enhanced our design capability incredibly. In the past two years we have even come to accept the truth of accepting the quality control truth that "none of us is as smart as all of us," and we have experimented—hesitantly at first—with participative management as a way of life that can make us more competitive in today's highly competitive world. We have investigated the ethnicity of various cultures, Japan being one example, as the *sine qua non* of success and have concluded that this is not a critical element.

With all the scientific advances we have made then, what is the critical spark that causes some organizations, some companies, some nations to succeed while others lag behind or fail? Is it resources, procedures, technology, homogeneity of culture, marketing, or just plain luck? While all of these elements may contribute in some way to success, I submit that there is an element which has been largely ignored in the area of quality and bringing about a *quality culture* which provides the competitive edge needed to put us in the winner's circle.

This missing foundation stone is *leadership*. This chapter will provide a background on the need for leadership, its origins, and ways it can be developed in organizations, whether manufacturing, service, or government. Does this sound too good to be true—or too simplistic to be valid? Take my word for it, it is neither. And it can be achieved.

### For Example

I was bonged aboard the flagship destroyer of my squadron. Since the occasion was a formal inspection, sideboys were present and the officer of the deck had meticulously inspected them to make certain that my first impression of the ship would be positive. I had heard the ship's public address system ring out with four strokes of the bell and the words, "Destroyer Squadron Nine arriving." It echoed over the calm sea as my gig made its approach.

The captain of the ship, in dress whites, white gloves, large medals, and sword, smiled as he observed that the quarterdeck was spotless and all equipment in place. My arrival was followed with an inspection tour that reflected the same attention to detail as my arrival. What a change from an inspection I had conducted on one of the other destroyers in my squadron. While obvious on the other ship that preparations for my inspection had been made, they fell far short of the results I witnessed on this flagship. Sloppy painting, gear adrift, and disinterested personnel were common.

What made the difference? Both skippers were Naval Academy graduates, both had a full complement of personnel, and the ships were the same vintage. The answer, of course, was in the *leadership* the captains exemplified. One had set his yardstick as "good enough was good enough." For the other, things had to be *completely* ready for a commodore's inspection. He was not the type of leader who called his executive officer and department heads into the wardroom, announced there was to be a squadron commander's inspection on Saturday, and then left the ship and the details to his officers. While he did not tell them *what* to do, his presence implied his interest and his support of what they were expected to do and encouraged their best efforts. They reacted accordingly.

The difference was *leadership*.

## FOUR TYPE OF LEADERS IN BUSINESS TODAY

My experience since retiring from the U.S. Navy in 1983 and rejoining corporate America has been that most U.S. executives fall into four general types of management styles. Consider your own organization and judge whether one of these descriptions doesn't fairly well describe your own management.

First, there still exists the *dinosaur*, the authoritarian type who says, "Do what I say without question. If you fail, we will find someone to replace you." This style of management led to the creation of unions, the we/they adversarial relationship between management and associates, the indifference to both external customers' desires and innovations by competitors, and eventually, market vulnerability.

Type two is the *transitional* manager. He or she has read and heard a great deal about the change in culture and the importance of quality. He or she may even have sent for the Malcolm Baldrige National Quality Award (MBNQA) criteria, then dismissed them as being impossible to achieve. This manager believes that change is necessary, but lacks sufficiently strong conviction to make a commitment.

Type three managers *understand* that the marketplace has changed, and realize that they and their organizations must also change. They hire consultants by the score, and enter the MBNQA competition not understanding that the award was established as competition against a set of criteria, not against other companies or that management quality would be one of the key factors in the judging. There are all levels of type three depending on degree of commitment. They all have one thing in common: a lack of understanding that change is achieved within the organization, and is not a magical metamorphosis brought about from the outside.

Type four I call the *perceptive, action-oriented manager.* He or she recognizes that an outside consultant is helpful in bringing certain organizational techniques of use in exploring shortcomings and needs, and perhaps providing more objective eyes. However, the problem solving and prioritizing of action *must be done by the organization*, which must drop business-as-usual attitudes long enough to see *itself* as its internal and external customers do and to devise a strategy by which it can gain a sustainable competitive advantage. The word *sustainable* is critical to the change.

## CHANGE—HAS IT OCCURRED? IF NOT, HOW DO WE BRING IT ABOUT?

Perhaps the Old Testament prophet Jeremiah gives us a clue from antiquity when he writes, "They have healed also the hurt of the daughter of my people slightly, saying, peace, peace: when there is no peace." (Jeremiah 6:14, KJV)

We have many today who announce that Communism is dead and that peace is now a done thing. True, the Berlin Wall is down and there is no gainsaying that the former USSR now resumes as the Confederation of Independent States (CIS) or Russia, a name discarded some three-quarters of a century ago. But does peace really reign and are there no countries now carrying the banner of communism? I believe the reader is able to answer that question with a resounding no. At the same time could any declare that prosperity is the predominant description of world economies? Ask yourself the question is *quality really* a way of life on planet Earth?

I would suggest that over the past decade we have introduced some new words and concepts into our lexicon, but have yet to grasp the true significance of these words compared to the results achieved.

Preparations for war, while having succeeded in bankrupting the Soviet Union, have left the industrialized nations—and I would emphasize the United States—in poor shape socially or economically to respond to the needs of countries emerging from the dark leadership of controlled economies. How will we respond to the unrest that now exists in so large a segment of the world's population? Is quality really the answer, or just a placebo that we toss carelessly about? If *quality is* the answer, how do we bring it about? Has change occurred? If not, how do we bring *it* about? I would suggest that change *is* occurring but at a far slower rate than many would have us believe. I am not convinced that the slow pace is due to a lack of documentation, which appears to be the straw we grasp as the answer to our current problem. I allude not to the lack of documentation confirmed by ISO 9000 or the Baldrige Award or various other national awards as the reason for the lack of rapid progress. I believe it is due in large part to our lack of understanding of the quality concept.

## QUALITY *IS* THE ANSWER

I believe that quality as a cultural *verity is* the answer to peace and prosperity in the world. I further believe that it can satisfy the needs and many of the desires of humankind. The major obstacle to this happening is the superficial understanding and thus judicious application of the meaning of *quality.*

This brings us to the question, how do we define quality for complete understanding? The British Standards Institution (BSi) defines *quality assurance* as "right first time" and *quality* as "fitness for purpose." Is this an adequate definition to describe the large number of factors responsible for achievement of quality? Do the terms total quality control (TQC), statistical process control (SPC), total quality management (TQM), or the U.S. Navy's current term, total quality leadership (TQL) simplify or complicate the process of understanding? Are any of these acronym-abused terms sufficiently comprehensive when submitted to a penetrating analysis?

In my judgment, we have darted from acronym to acronym trying to find the magic words that could bring success without either total understanding of the nature of our problem or the commitment required to achieve our objective. If asked what your opinion of the problem was, how would you answer? At the risk of being called arrogant, I would suggest that the core of our problem deals with people. Consider the theme of the conference to which I alluded at the beginning of this chapter: Peace and Prosperity, bringing them about through quality. For whom do we create this paradise? For *people*, of course. Who will bring it about? *People!* Who will judge the success of this *undertaking? People!* How widespread will this change necessarily have to occur to be successful? And herein lies another obstacle. I maintain it will need to occur in *all* of our institutions: government, management, religious and social organizations, labor force, professions. And it *must* have its start in the family, the basic unit where values are established. In short, we must change the cultural standards we now use to measure the value of work, the concept of responsibility, the importance of attitude, and the unquestionable need for accountability.

I would stipulate that quality is *not* a phantom, elusive dream we have pursued but never achieved. Instead, the failure has occurred in our lack of understanding of the concept.

Have I painted too dark a picture of our failures and too complex a picture of requirements for success?

## POSITIVE ASPECTS OF PROGRESS ACHIEVED THUS FAR

The ISO 9000 series is the current standards star. Whereas MIL-Q-9858A and MIL-I-45208 held the spotlight internationally for a number of decades, ISO 9000 is the darling of organizations desiring to do business internationally. Other than the make-work detail that it goes into, I have no problem with the described purpose of ISO 9000. I must confess that as quality czar for the U.S. Department of Defense from 1981 to 1983 I had no problem with MIL-Q-9858A as a QA management system either.

Metrology likewise has been highly developed over the years, to the point that we can measure our product to determine its compliance with this aspect of the specifications. Computer-aided design and manufacturing are additional tools which makes us more competitive from a time and option standpoint. Who can deny that visibility brought about by the prolific use of the term we call quality in advertising and the media has not been helpful? I can recall a decade ago, when we at the Defense Logistics Agency were hosting our Bottom-line Academia series, the paucity of courses about quality offered by U.S. colleges and universities. This was a particularly glaring discrepancy in the curricula of business institutions such as Harvard, Stanford, and Columbia universities. In the Madison Avenue marketing arena, the focus was on price for goods and services; today the watchword is *quality*. Authoritarian management and an emphasis on job security were the tenets my generation accepted for employment. Today the value of people working together for a common goal is being increasingly accepted as the magnet that attracts and holds people's interest in their jobs.

The insignificance of ethnic culture as a factor in quality has been established as I have compared the productivity and quality of products of American workers under Japanese management techniques to those of Japanese workers. We are beginning to realize that buzzwords, acronyms, and consultants are *not* the answer to a cultural change. We now, I believe, conclude that the brevity of top management's attention span is a negative factor in achieving significant change, and while resources, technology, marketing, timing, and luck play a part in competitive advantage, they are in no way the *sine qua non* of building a sustainable competitive advantage. May I suggest that these positive factors may represent the approaches to the bridge we are building—the bridge to peace and prosperity in our time.


## SO, WHAT'S NEXT?

Can we agree that the load-carrying capacity and longevity of a bridge rest principally on design and foundation? If so, then let us also accept the hypothesis that process control, design of experiments, inspection, testing and failure analysis are design features that, again, we have fairly well mastered. Now, let's examine what I consider the most important element of our bridge design, the foundation! This foundation, be it piling, pontoon, pier, or suspension, is usually dictated by location, and length and composition of support substance. I suggest that in the bridge we are building we postulate that *leadership* is the key foundation element.


## EXAMINING THE FOUNDATION WE CALL LEADERSHIP

If leadership *is* the essential element for success in establishing quality as the bridge to peace and prosperity, we must first define it and then decide how we implement it.

### Defining Leadership
The Second College Edition of the *American Heritage Dictionary* defines *leader* as follows: "one that leads or guides; one in charge or in command of others; one who has influence or power [as in political power]; a conductor of an orchestra."

**Describing Leadership**

Holy Scriptures have some interesting and apt descriptions of what a leader does to establish authority:

> "I will go *before* you to make the crooked places straight; I will break in pieces the gates of brass and cut asunder the bars of iron."
>
> (Isaiah 45:2)

> ". . .Yea though I walk through the valley of the shadow of death, I will fear no evil for *thou* art with *me*; thy rod and thy staff they comfort me. . ."
>
> (The famous Psalm 23:4 of King David)

Do *your* leaders fit either of these descriptions? Do *they* go *before you* to make the crooked paths straight, do they clear the way of constraints or help you identify them? Regardless of the economic tempest we are experiencing, do your leaders give you the confidence that they will lead you through it safely? Do your managers lead or guide you? Do they, like the conductor of a great symphony orchestra, orchestrate the process of change that will cause your company to achieve a sustainable competitive advantage? Or are they *too busy* to provide that kind of hands-on leadership?

A number of years ago, while a student at the U.S. Naval War College in Newport, Rhode Island, I was having lunch with a close friend and Officer Candidate School classmate of mine. Tom was a naval aviator, I was a black shoe or ship driver. I was headed for command of a destroyer, he was in his tour as an F-4 fighter squadron commander and had just returned from a deployment in the western Pacific off Vietnam. I asked Tom how he enjoyed being a squadron commander. He replied that this was what he had joined the Navy to be. I queried him about his duties: "I presume that you make out the sortie schedule and then watch your people take off on their mission."

"No, Frank," he replied, "I don't *see* them off, I *lead* them off!" In 11 succinct words, Commander Tom Wimberly had described what leadership is all about.

The recent transition of the Israel Defense Force's leadership school for infantry cadets from transactional to transformational leadership is another case of keying in on the crucial aspects of leadership. Leadership, to be effective, *must be transformational, not transactional*, in nature if it is to create officers capable of inspiring men to dedicate their last full measure of devotion to unit and country. This aspect of leadership may be applied to any organization.

My own definition of a leader, forged from 33 years' experience in war and peace in the U.S. Navy is "a person, working through and with people, who inspires them to perform beyond their individual motivation, or at times *well above* their capabilities."

## NINE QUALITIES OF A LEADER

General "Stormin' Norman" Schwarzkopf, U.S. Army commander and hero of Operation Desert Storm, following his retirement developed a motivational tape for industry leaders entitled *Take Charge.* In it, he listed seven important qualities of a leader. Therefore, I share them and add two more, giving the nine marks that I believe distinguish a leader.

### 1. Leaders Help People Succeed
Too often nowadays managers are reluctant to help people succeed for fear they might displace them. My theory has always been that the better your associates look and the more capability they demonstrate, the better the leader looks.

### 2. Don't Consider Management with Leadership. They Differ Vastly!
While leaders are often good managers (they must be to have the resources in place to support success) managers need not be good leaders to succeed. Management keys on managing material resources, while leaders key on *people.*

### 3. Set Goals That Everyone Can Understand, and State Them Simply
Verbose, complex goals confuse and discourage understanding. As a result, people fail to buy in.

### 4. Set High Standards: "Good Enough" is Not Good Enough!
Anything short of the highest standards of behavior and effort will fail to achieve success in today's competitive arena, whether it be business or battlefield. The leader must ensure that he or she meets these standards.

### 5. There Is Always Room for Improvement
Anyone complacent enough to accept the comfort of status quo is in for a rude awakening. He or she will be run over by the competition. Dr. Deming's constant improvement as a mind-set is essential, not only for the leader, but also for his associates. They must be encouraged to seek constantly how things can be improved, both procedures and product.

### 6. A Leader Must Take Charge

Taking charge means just that. Stepping up to responsibility and account-ability, having a plan, and being decisive in implementing it are part and parcel of the baggage a leader is expected to carry. Associates can sense indecisiveness, and leaders will soon find themselves displaced or attempt-ing to cope with indecisiveness throughout the organization.

### 7. Do What Is Right

This is not nearly as easy to do as it is to say. What is right? Understanding of this is normally the product of a well-grounded set of values. Without socially accepted principles, a leader will find himself or herself floundering as he or she seeks a consensus of what is right. While we have examples of world leaders who have been guided by anything but right moral values, their historical legacy has seldom been one of adulation.

### 8. Give Credit Where Credit Is Due

Another common failing is to feel that, having taken all the risks, you should gain all the credit. Bear in mind, no leader is ever responsible for the total success of any plan. While his or her genius may have laid the founda-tion, the bricks and mortar are always the products of their associates' efforts.

### 9. Demonstrate the Virtue of Loyalty

Loyalty both up and down are essential virtues of a successful leader. Impossible, you say? Not if you keep everyone informed. Trying to make your boss the scapegoat for an unpopular outcome can have disastrous effects and will erode any loyalty your associates have for you.

If we now have a concise mind's-eye picture of what a leader does and what leadership is all about—and bear in mind that quality is for, by, and with people—what is the litmus test for determining a person's (even our own) capacity for leadership?

## TEN CRITERIA OF LEADERSHIP

If you desire to see how close you come to having the leadership capabilities that portend success ask yourself the following questions. Or, if you prefer, determine whether your leader fulfills the following criteria.

### 1. Effectively Articulating Goals

Do you articulate effectively the shared goals that you desire to be achieved to attain a sustainable competitive advantage? Put another way, do you make clear the "What's in it for us?" (WIIFU) versus "What's in it for me?" (WIIFM) of the change you wish to implement in the way you are now doing business? This is a most important element to have in hand *before* suggesting change to subordinates. It will be the first question in their minds when you suggest change.

### 2. Understanding of Needs of Customers

Do you have a firm understanding of the needs and desires of both your internal and external customers, the approach and success of your chief competitors, and the capabilities, authority, and resources you have to work with? Without this knowledge, how can you hope to orchestrate the change you have in mind?

### 3. Planning for Achieving Goals

Have you established a detailed plan of achievement and determined how best to present it to your subordinates, your superiors, and your shareholders? The *how* will be the second question asked of you by those you hope to lead into the battle for change.

### 4. Nurturing a Team Mentality

How adept are you at nurturing a team mentality, ensuring that there are no *unimportant* people in your plan of action. If anyone's contribution is unimportant, then there is little need for that person on the team. Bear in mind, your subordinates must have confidence that, not only is it to *their* benefit to be involved, but also that the plan can succeed and that their contributions are both significant and noteworthy.

### 5. Identifying Constraints

Have you honestly identified the constraints now discernible, and will you understand how to solve those that may later appear? While it is generally impossible to ferret out *all* the problems that may arise, you must be aware of as many as possible to respond when subordinates or superiors point them out during the course of carrying out your plan.

### 6. Providing a Positive Example of Leadership

Leadership demands inspiration through a positive personal example. An old adage describes it concisely: "What you do speaks so loud that I can't hear what you are saying." The acronym MBWA/AQ, management by walking around and asking questions, is pertinent. "Don't tell me, show me" is the reaction of today's associates. If getting to work on time is important to success, be punctual yourself. If you want to establish a real team spirit, walk around the floor of your organization, learn the names of your people, see what their personal aspirations and goals are and how they think the business can be improved. Does this take time? The answer is yes, but success is a time-consuming taskmaster!

### 7. Taking Risks
Are you willing to take risks and supply the resources needed for success, including that most costly of all resources, your time and the time of others in your organization? Risk taking does not mean being foolhardy, but to be successful in today's market arena requires sticking your neck out and laying it on the line when necessary. Face it. Getting out of bed and driving to work each day requires a degree of risk. Life itself is a risk. There is no guarantee of complete and inviolate safety. The resource issue is extremely important, for once you have your locomotive or steamboat or stock car moving, it is essential that you don't run out of fuel before achieving your objective. To do so means a most difficult if not impossible task of regenerating interest, enthusiasm, and credibility for change.

### 8. Maintaining Persistence
Do you have a mind-set that persistence, even more than intellect, has been responsible for success in efforts upon which you are embarking? The perversion of the motto, "If at first you don't succeed, try, try again," to "If at first you don't succeed, give up," has been the downfall of many worthy goals. And while how you play the game is important, *winning is also very important.* Otherwise there would be no reason to keep score.

### 9. Delegating Effectively
Do you find it easy to delegate, to share responsibility at the lowest responsible level? And do you hold people accountable when you have given them the opportunity to grow through shared responsibility? Do you hold *yourself* accountable for failures and honestly admit failure and take failure's consequences? There are no "golden parachutes" for failures in the contest for survival and success.

**10. Pressing On**

Finally, I would borrow from one of the great leaders of World War II, who concluded his speech to cadets at the famous British military school, Sandhurst, by saying, "Men, I leave you with three cardinal rules for success on the battlefield: Never give up, never give up, never, never give up!" The man, of course, was Winston Churchill.

## THE NEEDS TODAY: LEADERS AND LEADERSHIP

Leadership is the fuse that ignites the inspiration and generates motivation to succeed. Without it, no amount of procedures or instructions will achieve competitive, particularly sustainable, competitive advantage.

The need today is for application of leadership principles by those in top and middle management and even first-line supervisor positions in manufacturing and service organizations. Further, we need people in top and key positions in government, church, and social organizations to possess, and govern their actions with, these same leadership principles. These principles—anchored in integrity, morality, vision, and action—can indeed be the foundation for the bridge to prosperity and peace that we require for economic survival and success in the twenty-first century.

What we need is more action, *not* more seminars and conferences: more *leaders*, fewer consultants. The need today is for *leadership* in management.

# EPILOGUE

When the United States engaged Spain and assisted Cuba in attaining its independence, President William McKinley needed to send a message to General Garcia, head of the revolutionary forces in Cuba. The exact whereabouts of General Garcia were unknown, except that he was somewhere in the jungles of Cuba.

Someone suggested sending a young army lieutenant named Andrew Summers Rowan. Lieutenant Rowan was summoned and given an oilskin pouch containing a message to Garcia. His instructions, put plainly and simply, were to deliver the pouch to General Garcia. The where, how, and when to deliver the message were left up to Rowan, who was put ashore on Cuba from an open boat. Disappearing into the jungle, he traversed the hostile jungle for three weeks and then reappeared, his mission completed.

While I would be immodest to compare myself to Lieutenant—and later Colonel—Rowan, within the pages of this book is also a message to Garcia. More accurately put, this message is to *all* the General Garcias who lead manufacturing and service industries. To these General Garcias I say, "Take heed."

The message is clear and has been delivered. The enemy has been identified: nonconformance to the customer's desires and requirements. The issue is *quality*.

Your challenge is to press home and *implement change*, so that the message in this book will be as effective as was the message to General Garcia from President McKinley via Lieutenant Rowan.

Perhaps the Old Testament book of Ecclesiastes says it even more succinctly: "Whatsoever thy hand findeth to do, do it with all thy might . . ." (Ecclesiastes 9:10, KJV).

# APPENDIX A: TYPES OF INDUSTRIES VISITED, 1981–1993

The visit breakdown shown here were visits made during my tour as quality czar for the DOD. Upon retirement, I joined Avco Corporation as corporate vice president for quality. Two years later, Avco was taken over by Textron. I made the transition, and held the same position in Textron that I did with Avco. During my tour as vice president of quality for both firms, I had the responsibility for bringing about a quality culture in some 26 divisions, including Avco Aerostructure, Avco Electronics, Avco Financial Services, Textron Financial Insurance Group, three aircraft engine groups, an Avco Management Services Division, Avco Research Laboratory, Avco Specialty Materials, Systems Division, Bell Aerospace, Bell Helicopter, Camcar, Cherry Fasteners, CWC Castings, EZ-Go Golf Carts, Gorham Silver, Homelite, HR Textron, Jacobsen, Paul Revere Insurance Group, Randall Automotive, Sheaffer Eaton, Textron Financial Corporation, Speidel, and Townsend Automotive Parts. This experience covered, as is obvious, a wide spectrum of high-tech military and consumer goods from M-1 tank engines and Peacekeeper Missile reentry vehicles to Gorham Silver and a wide variety of insurance.

In 1985, while still with Textron, I made a three-week trip to China with an ASQC people-to-people group where we visited Beijing, Tianjin, Dalian, Shenyang, and Guanqzhou. In these major industrial cities we lectured to a spectrum of middle managers and first-line supervisors that crossed many industries. In 1987, I left Textron to form my own international quality consultancy and have conducted quality culture changing training in companies in the United States, Israel, and Hong Kong under my own aegis as a private consultant, Frank Collins Associates Survival Twenty-One. From these experiences, I have gained the insights I share between the covers of this book.

I have revisited Japan and Korea since my original data-gathering trips and have attempted to update the data I gathered and analyzed before retiring. In some cases the data are the original collected in 1981 through 1983. I've not disturbed it in such cases since I believe the purpose of my book has been to demonstrate how the Far East and industrial giants in manufacturing were using quality to achieve a competitive edge! The data, I believe, are still useful from that perspective.

| Product Breakdown | % |
|---|---|
| Space/aircraft | 10 |
| Level 1/subsafe/nuclear power | 10 |
| Heavy machinery (e.g., tanks) | 10 |
| Aircraft components | 7 |
| Truck/car manufacturing | 7 |
| Weapons systems (radar and sonar electronic warfare) | 5 |
| Missiles | 5 |
| Electronics (chip) | 5 |
| Electronics (precision instruments) | 5 |
| Miscellaneous | 5 |
| Clothing, textile, and shoes | 4 |
| Ammunition | 4 |
| Electrical (general) | 4 |
| Communications equipment | 3 |
| Light machine manufacturing | 3 |
| Ordnance | 2 |
| Aircraft overhaul | 2 |
| Metal manufacturing | 2 |
| Shipbuilding | 2 |
| Aircraft parts (distributor) | 2 |
| Training simulator | 1 |
| A/C manufacturing, petroleum, robotics, computer, camera, optical | < 1 each |

# APPENDIX B: COMPUTING THE COST OF NONCONFORMANCE (CON)

## COST OF NONCONFORMANCE

$$CNC = \frac{S + WO + RR_1 + RR_2 + CA + IE + PMC}{B}$$

$CNC$ = Cost of Nonconformance
$S$ = Scrap
$WO$ = Work Omission
$RR_1$ = Rework and Repair
$RR_2$ = Reinspection and Retest
$CA$ = Corrective Action
$IE$ = Inventory Excess to compensate for parts/product failure required to meet delivery schedule
$PMC$ = Postmanufacturing Cost
$B$ = Base (For trend monitoring, this should be in constant dollars.)

**Note:** All variables are in dollars. All labor costs are to have burden applied.

### Definitions of Variables
1. Scrap

- Replacement cost of item (product, part, material, tool, software) at point of loss consisting of:

  Labor (manufacturing, quality, planning, scheduling)

  plus

  Cost of productivity lost due to rescheduling or resequencing factory and equipment (cost of additional equipment or tooling setups, cost

181

of additional factory and equipment carried due to known or expected nonconformances, cost of nonavailability of factory and equipment for normal production, other costs of doing work out of sequence)

plus

Cost of capital associated with loss of productivity

## 2. Work Omissions

- Reprocessing cost due to nonconformance to requirements because of missed or partially completed operations or activities
- Cost of productivity lost due to rescheduling or resequencing factory and equipment (as under Scrap)
- Cost of capital associated with loss of productivity

## 3. Rework and Repair

(Note: While some consider R&R, as a possible cost increase times two, I would suggest it is closer to a **x3** factor since while you are doing R&R on the original product, those people/machines are *not* being utilized for original production.)

- Cost of total manufacturing labor expended to reduce severity of or eliminate nonconformances
- Labor cost of planners or schedulers and others involved
- Cost of work stations added in manufacturing sequence to perform rework due to low process yields
- Internal cost for correcting supplier deficiencies
- Cost of rework effort included in standards for task accomplishment
- Cost of additional material required
- Cost of activities as above due to engineering changes (other than customer-required design changes) or technical data errors
- Cost for correcting spares and spares provisioning data
- Expenses and travel required
- Cost of productivity lost due to rescheduling or resequencing factory and equipment (as under Scrap)
- Cost of overtime expended

4. Reinspection and Retest ($R\&R_2$)

- Cost of quality assurance or control efforts resulting from other events (scrap, work omissions, rework, repair, etc.)
- Cost of required support personnel such as test equipment operators
- Cost of additional screening or inspection effort to detect or remove same or similar conditions
- Cost of any manufacturing labor that operates inspection points as pre-screening activity
- Cost of overtime expended in order to meet scheduled delivery date

5. Corrective Action

- Administrative cost of operating material review activity and corrective action systems including labor costs of personnel (quality, engineering, manufacturing, clerical, other)
- Cost of failure investigation and analysis of both hardware and software (including embedded software) nonconformances including time of source quality, engineering, and purchasing representatives were applicable
- Engineering time required to correct design or drawing errors including software design and programming errors
- Labor and administrative cost of processing engineering and data changes due to design or human error through the configuration management activity
- Labor and administrative cost of correcting or revising manufacturing and inspection procedures or instructions
- Internal labor cost (purchasing, manufacturing, quality, engineering, other) to obtain replacement procedures or instructions
- Cost of correcting defective numerical control tapes
- Cost of waivers and deviations, including all processing costs

6. Inventory Excess

- Cost of additional stock carried due to known or expected nonconforming parts or material (both purchased and manufactured in advance of needs)
- Cost of capital charge associated with excess stock

- Cost of expedited deliveries to meet artificially created, earlier-than-necessary need dates

7. Postmanufacturing Cost

- Warranty cost of returned products
- Cost of field service effort in lieu of returns (labor, expenses, travel)
- Cost to retrofit nonconforming material
- Cost of lost product utility, longevity, reliability, and maintainability of use-as-is material
- Software cost

8. Base

Total manufacturing direct labor dollars (including overhead) in constant dollars

## Quality Systems: Measure of Effectiveness*

- Quality operations (cost as percent of total operating cost)
- Supplier component rejection rate (numerical as well as dollar value percent of total purchase increased cost to remedy)
- Engineering design changes (those essential for producibility after initial submission for production)
- Number of material review board actions, requests for deviation, and requests for waiver (each as a percentage of the number of different products produced)
- Scrap, rework, and repair as percent of total manufacturing costs
- Returns (scrap, rework, other costs)
- Warranty action (cost to repair or replace)

---

* While quality *is* free, if having been factored into initial cost of design, production, and warranty, our lack of acceptance of the quality culture concept has caused us to add a surcharge which we label "quality." It is thus important that we measure the effectiveness of this surcharge rather than just accept it as a new cost of doing business. Otherwise, we have raised our cost of production without justifiably improving our competitive advantages.

# APPENDIX C:
# QUALITY DEFINITIONS
# AND IMPLICATIONS
# FROM ANTIQUITY
# TO THE PRESENT

On quality, an ancient discipline:

> "If a builder constructed a house, but did not make his work strong, with the result that the house which he built collapsed and caused the death of the owner of the house, the builder shall be put to death!"
>
> Article 234
> Code of Hammurabi
> Circa 1600 B.C.

On quality, as prescribed in antiquity:

> "If a boatman caulked a boat for a seigneur and did not do the boat well with the result that the boat has sprung a leak in that very year, since it has developed a defect, the boatman shall dismantle that boat and strengthen it at his own expense."
>
> Article 229
> Code of Hammurabi
> Circa 1600 B.C.

During the time of Apostle Paul, quality was an issue:

> "And this I pray, that your love may abound yet more and more in knowledge and in all judgment; that ye may approve things that are excellent, and that ye may be sincere and without offense till the day of Christ."
>
> Philippians 1: 9–10

On director's guidance:

> "My philosophy on how we are to do our job? It is merely this: *We must be so thorough that the only way we will permit the delivery of any product of poor quality is to be overruled by someone who is authorized to accept that responsibility.* I am personally committed to this philosophy; I ask you to do no less; and I assure you of my support."*
>
> E. A. Grinstead
> Vice Admiral, SC, USN
> Director, DLA

On Britain's national campaign for quality:

> "The government believes that *quality* is the business of every member of the work force, and particularly that of top management. Chief executives must take the lead and make quality a *personal* responsibility."
>
> Lord Cockfield
> Britain's Secretary of State for Trade

On the issues of quality and productivity:

> "Following the examples of our forebears, we need to rely on basics, yet dare to dream, always remembering that there is *no* substitute for quality. Excellence must never be compromised."
>
> President Ronald Reagan
> August 20, 1984

## Quality Defined

> "Quality is *everyone* trying to do a better job, make a better effort at whatever he is doing in order to improve his performance and improve Avco's performance for *our customers*. We are looking for everyone to think in terms of how *I* can do it differently, how can *I* do it better to achieve total performance, and because of this, we as individuals get better *job satisfaction* from doing so."
>
> Robert B. Bauman
> Chairperson of the Board
> Avco Corporation

*\*QA Reporter* NR 43.

"Let there be *no doubt* that all of us mean what we say when we define quality for Avco as *defect free* and *doing it right the first time.* There is nothing more important than achieving our *quality objective* and maintaining the drive required to *institutionalize Avco's quality culture.*"

> Donald K. Farrar
> President and Chief Operating Officer
> Avco Corporation

"Quality control does not mean achieving perfection. It means the efficient production of the quality that the market expects."

> W. Edwards Deming
> Quality Consultant

"Quality is an achievable, measurable, profitable entity that can be installed once you have commitment and understanding and are prepared for hard work."

> Philip B. Crosby
> Chairperson
> Philip Crosby Associates

"Quality is an attitude and a personal commitment to excellence. Quality is also our strongest competitive weapon."

> Douglas D. Danforth
> Chairprson
> Westinghouse Electric Corporation

"Quality is our best assurance of customer allegiance, our strongest defense against foreign competition, and the only path to sustained growth and earnings."

> John F. Welch, Jr.
> Chief Executive Officer
> General Electric Company

"Also of considerable importance, in my judgment, is the sense of personal pride and esteem that grows out of a quality effort . . ."

> L. W. Lehr
> Chairperson
> 3M Corporation

"As quality goes up, so does productivity. Consider the impact on overall levels of productivity—if everyone and every machine performed properly the first time, every time."

William M. Conway
Chairperson
Nashua Corporation

"Quality is what the customer perceives when he feels that a product meets his needs and lives up to his expectations."

W. R. Thurston
President and CEO
GenRad Corporation

## Quality of Life

"Live neither in the past nor in the future, but let each day's work absorb all your interest, energy, and enthusiasm. The best preparation for tomorrow is to do today's work superbly well."

Sir William Osler

"Live one day at a time, and make it a masterpiece."

Anonymous

"It's a funny thing about life . . . if you refuse to accept anything but the best, you very often get it."

W. Somerset Maugham

## Quotations on Quality from the Bottom-Line II Conference (Washington, D.C.: June 1, 1983)

"High quality in weapons and military equipment will be possible only when the chief executive of the producing company has a strong personal commitment to it."

David Packard
Chairperson of the Board
Hewlett-Packard Company

"Many industries have accepted as normal a 15 percent scrap rate for their products as compared with a scrap rate of 1 percent in Japan."

> J. M. Juran
> Chairperson
> Juran Institute

"Attitude is the critical issue."

> William J. Weisz
> Chief Operating Officer
> Motorola

"The navy should be more patient in not insisting on production of a weapon before it is ready. We need a working, reliable, mature system when it gets there."

> Admiral Sylvester Foley, USN
> Commander in Chief, U.S. Pacific Fleet

"We have been deficient in defining what our requirements are."

> General P. X. Kelly
> USMC
> Asst. Commandant

"The cost of correcting defects in weapons runs in the range of 10 to 30 percent of the cost of each weapon. This represents enormous waste—billions of dollars."

> Paul Thayer
> Deputy Secretary of Defense

# APPENDIX D: EXAMPLES OF QUALITY POLICY STATEMENTS*

## PERFECTION'S QUALITY POLICY

The Perfection Company is dedicated to the manufacture of high-quality, reliable products that meet the needs defined by our customers.

Achieving customer requirements, as defined by specifications, is the responsibility of all Perfection employees.

## THE BIG Q

Providing customers with what they want, when they want it, at the promised price.

## QUALITY POLICY

Our company policy is

- To provide our customers with products and services that meet or exceed their expectations.
- To provide employees with a desirable work environment, competitive remuneration, and a satisfying personal challenge.
- To provide our stockholders with a competitive rate of return on investment and an image of competence and long-term stability.

*Note: All quality policy statements should be signed by the chief executive officer and distributed to all employees.

191

To achieve these goals, we need a high level of dedication from *all* employees and suppliers to perform all aspects of their tasks as completely and as thoroughly as they know how and to seek to improve all aspects of the organization for our mutual benefit.

## XYZ QUALITY POLICY

We, as XYZ employees, commit to designing, manufacturing, delivering, and servicing quality products and services that meet or exceed our customer's expectations.

# APPENDIX E: SUGGESTED INDUSTRY-SPONSORED INITIATIVES TO IMPROVE QUALITY

1. Explore increased application of statistics in the design stage of projects to determine probability of success in design-production transition.

2. Industries and trade associations endow quality chairs at select business and engineering institutions.

3. Establish a task force of industry procurement contracting officers, project managers, and DCAS representatives to develop QA techniques for implementation in new product development phase.

4. Support the establishment of a President's Quality Award to be presented annually to those companies meeting established criteria in areas of quality ranging from published policy to product excellence.

5. Establish within each industry quality goals and standards as a means of measuring quality improvement.

6. Organize a joint industry/DOD committee to devise standard contract forms to achieve greater uniformity of content and ease of understanding.

7. Have companies who have experienced major improvements in quality, volunteer to be Harvard Business School case studies so that other industries will have an opportunity to recognize the positive impact that quality can have on profit and productivity.

8. Top managers of companies with successful quality improvement programs can offer to conduct seminars at leading business schools on management's role in and responsibility for improving quality.

9. Company engineers and managers could become involved with local educational institutions, to ensure the continuation of courses being taught in the quality field, by auditing school classes and curricula.

10. Give your top engineers sabbaticals to teach in a university setting so they can bring an updated understanding of production and quality problems to the attention of future engineers.

11. Develop an organization—comprising industry, academic, scientific, engineering, and management communities—similar to JUSE to solve quality problems. Publish results and establish training programs to ensure quality awareness and understanding from the top down in the industrial and white-collar communities.

12. Promote a quality leadership policy within industry that is oriented toward product reliability rather than warranty.

# APPENDIX F: A SHORT QUALITY LEXICON

*Availability:* The readiness of a product or system to perform as designed, meeting or exceeding the predicted mean time between failure (MTBF) and mean time before maintenance procedure (MTBMP).

*Cost of Nonconformance (CNC):* The cost associated with scrap, repair, rework, retest, reinspection, material review board (MRB), warranty claims, field reps, lost business, complaint adjudication, and all the other elements properly connected with satisfying the customer (at times mislabeled Cost of Quality).

*Customer:* Anyone to whom you provide a service or product or to whom you add value in a multiprocess product or service.

*Customer Quality:* Meeting not only a customer's specification standards, but in addition, his expectations, on time and at the agreed-upon price.

*Design Quality:* The ability to design a product that, using available, equipment, facilities, personnel, techniques, and procedures, will meet the customer's desires.

*Inspection:* Ascertaining, by visual, electronic, or mechanical means, the achievement of the customer's specifications for a manufactured product.

*Nonconformance:* The lack of process control that produces unacceptable material requiring scrapping, rework, repair, or MRB, or customer waivers for acceptance.

195

*Process Control:* The ability, primarily through use of various control charts, to ascertain when a manufacturing process is within acceptable limits, and alarm need for corrective action, when necessary in order to avoid need for rework, repair, or scrapping an otherwise unacceptable product. Such process control may also be used in nonmanufacturing situations.

*Productivity:* The effective design and utilization of all factors essential to a market-satisfying manufacturing or service-providing operation. This includes, but is not limited to, customer interface, functional integration of personnel and equipment, utilization of current technology, training, facilities, positive attitude, identity with associated product and organization, and recognition of the customer as the company's reason for being. It is a combination of commitment and attitude of constant improvement. A second viable definition was articulated by the Japanese productivity agency when I visited then in 1965. Above all, an attitude of mind, an attitude of progress, of the constant improvement of what exists. It is the certainty of being able to do better today than yesterday, and less well than tomorrow. It is the will to improve on the present situation, no matter how good it may seem, no matter how good it may really be. It is the constant adaption of economic and social life to changing conditions. It is the continual effort to apply new techniques and new methods. It is faith in human progress. (AKA European Productivity Agency [1965]).

*Quality:* The ability of all organizational processes to deliver a product or service that meets the needs and expectations of internal and external customers in a productive fashion and at a cost that represents a good value. It is an attitude of the importance of what we do; it is a positive philosophy of life. The short version: Value to the customer, profit to the producer, and satisfaction to both.

*Quality Assurance (QA):* A quality system that extends from design to purchasing to manufacturing to test and evaluation and contains an effective interface with customer and supplier to assure that the customer's specifications and expectations are met or exceeded.

*Quality Control (QC):* The systematic oversight during the manufacturing and production phase that promotes achievement of the desired product or service.

*Quality Culture:* An environment in which work and effort are revered as being necessary for human existence and progress, one in which each person believes that "doing the right thing right, the first time and on time" is the norm and is important not only for the customer's acceptance, but also the supplier's job satisfaction. It is the belief that each and every person in the process is important, and that team action is the only logical way to achieve the common goal of sustainable competitive advantage. It includes a participative and supportive management, a trained, motivated, and well-led work force and a totally functional-integrated infrastructure.

*Quality-Productivity Interface:* Quality is doing right things right, productivity is doing it right the first time.

*Reliability:* The ability of a product to meet or exceed the design and customer's expectations for operation and availability within the design, specifications, and prescribed maintenance procedures.

*Supplier:* Anyone who provides you with a service or product or who adds value to a process or service in advance of your receipt.

*Supplier Quality:* The ability of a supplier to meet the quality standards of customers (the end user's needs) in its material or component.

*Sustainable Competitive Advantage:* The continuing ability to control and profit from a growing segment of the market for which a service or product is designed.

*Total Quality Management (TQM):* The totality of effort and organization that includes management's active participation, support, and vision and sensitivity to both the market and to internal customers; the functional interaction of all elements involved in bringing a product or service to market and providing postsale support and recognition and reward of those whose contributions are above normal expectations.

# APPENDIX G: ESSENTIAL ELEMENTS OF ISO 9000

**ISO 9000**
Series of international standards for quality identical to BS 5750 and EN 29000

**Basic Definitions**
QA: right first time
Quality: fitness for purpose

**Documentational Requirements**
Level one: Statement of policy
Level two: Procedures for implementing policy
Level three: Task instructions for specific activities

**ISO 9001**
Specification for design, development, production, installation, and servicing

**ISO 9002**
Specification for production and installation

**ISO 9003**
Specification for final inspection and testing

**ISO 9001 Quality System Model**
4.1   Management Responsibility
4.2   Quality System
4.3   Contract Review
4.4   Design Control

4.5   Document Control
4.6   Purchasing
4.7   Purchaser Supplied Products
4.8   Product Identification and Traceability
4.9   Process Control
4.10  Inspection and Testing
4.11  Inspection, Measuring, and Test Equipment
4.12  Inspection and Test Status
4.13  Control of Nonconforming Product
4.14  Corrective Action
4.15  Handling, Storage, Packaging, and Delivery
4.16  Quality Records
4.17  Internal Quality Audits
4.18  Training
4.19  Servicing
4.20  Statistical Techniques

**ISO 9002 Omits**
4.4   Design Control
4.19  Servicing

**ISO 9003**
Includes only 12 of 20. Quality assured by testing and inspection (product or service quite simple).

**General Requirements of ISO 9000**

- Management commitment
- Defined responsibilities
- Complete written statement of policy and objectives, procedures and detailed instructions, and control information
- Regular internal audits of system
- Assurance that employees have skills, qualifications, and training appropriate to their tasks.

# APPENDIX H: THE MALCOLM BALDRIGE NATIONAL QUALITY AWARD: A DREAM REALIZED*

"But America's economic strength lies first and foremost in our ability to innovate—through technology, managerial commitment and labor's skill—and to improve productivity and *quality*. I can think of no better way for us to seize this opportunity for growth than a new focus on the *quality* of our products and services." These were the words with which Honorable Ronald Reagan, the President of the United States, on March 31, 1988, initiated America's most prestigious recognition for any company which wins the honor, and the most important beginning for any company that applies and is serious about changing the culture of their organization by focusing on the Malcolm Baldrige National Quality Award criteria as the change vehicle for their own organization. But this was hardly the beginning.

The birth of the Malcolm Baldrige National Quality Award actually began in 1982 when as executive director of quality assurance for the Defense Logistics Agency (the Department of Defense's (DOD) contract administrator for all the services), I made a trip to Japan to see for myself why the Japanese were succeeding so well in the international marketplace, especially in the United States. As the DOD's quality czar, I had some small measure of influence on the 16,000 defense contractors who depended on our quality assurance representatives to sign off on the DD 250 forms which authorized payment for the goods or services they provided. Since this amounted to over $50 billion annually, it served as an attention getter when I visited our defense contractors, and I normally had an opportunity to sit down with the chairperson, president, and general manager to discover their philosophy on, and participation in, the organization's quality process. I

---

*By Frank C. Collins Jr. Reprinted from the April 1989 issue of *Quality Digest*, P.O. Box 882, Red Bluff, CA 96080. © 1989 QCI international. All rights reserved.

hoped that the trip would equip me to share some of the reasons for Japanese success with these executives, many of whom became very defensive when compared to Japanese managers.

My visits to Japan in 1982 and 1983, which included Korea, were time well spent. I discovered the Japanese proclivity for production and their passion for perfection. As I visited companies such as Yokogowa Hewlett-Packard, Komatsu, NKK Steel, Tokyo Juki, and many other Deming Prize winners, I was struck by the value that these companies placed on winning the Deming Prize. I recalled the half page ad in the *Wall Street Journal* in the fall of 1981 displaying a large cut of the Deming Prize medal with words below it which read, "The most important name in Japanese quality control is American." The ad was run by Sumitomo Metals, which had won the coveted honor in 1953—some 28 years earlier.

"Why can't America have a national quality award?" I thought to myself. "Do we need such an initiative? Why certainly! America has a very competitive spirit. It should serve to motivate companies to achieve the excellence of which we are capable." This was the way I played the idea in my mind all the way back to the States.

My first thought was, it should not be a political football. Therefore, why not suggest that some prestigious organization *outside* of the government sponsor it. "The National Academy of Sciences (NAS) would be perfect," I reasoned. "Prestigious, super relationship with the industrial community as well as academe and the professional societies." The chief of my technical division, Col. Bob Dunderville, USAF, had been on loan to the National Academy of Sciences in a previous tour and knew some of the leaders. He offered to introduce me to them and see how they would react.

NAS reacted enthusiastically. They promised to get some of their CEOs together and spring it on them. Then, depending on their reaction, they would schedule a brainstorming session on how best to implement the concept. Regrettably, three months later we were told that the CEOs with whom they had raised the issue responded negatively, stating "the academy already sponsored enough awards." The lyrics, "How can something which seems so right, be so wrong," ran through my mind as I received this news.

Establishing contact with Dr. Myron Tribus, noted engineer, educator, and confidante of Dr. Deming, I asked him what could be done, after explaining what we had attempted. Myron, ex-assistant secretary of commerce for Science and Technology, indicated that the Department of Commerce should be the next stop. Subsequently I spoke to Dr. Bruce Merrifield, who at the time was assistant secretary of commerce for

Productivity, Technology, and Innovation. Bruce was also enthusiastically in favor of the concept, but when it was briefed to the President's Council of Economic Advisors, the briefer failed to get a positive response. All this occurred during 1982 and 1983, and left me somewhat discouraged that the leaders in business and government in America could be so indifferent to an idea whose time, in my mind, had definitely come.

In October of 1983, President Reagan created the White House Conference on Productivity Act by signing PL 97-367, which directed leaders from industry, academe, and the professions to look into the decline of U.S. productivity. I was privileged to be a member of the private sector study that would establish the relationship between quality and productivity. Dr. C. Jackson Grayson, then president and CEO, now chairperson and CEO of the American Productivity/Quality Center in Houston chaired the Private Sector Initiatives Panel, which encompassed the quality subpanel.

This latter committee, composed of a number of quality professionals and educators, established a computer network that allowed users to exchange ideas regarding the essential role quality must play in improving America's productivity. I shared with this group the efforts to create interest in establishing a national quality award. This cadre of quality professionals by and large endorsed the idea. I was most disappointed when the White House Conference on Productivity convened at the State Department in Washington, D.C., September 21–25, 1983 (just three weeks after I had retired from 33 years' active duty in the U.S. Navy) to report the results to the president, and discovered that in the final written report to the president, there was no recommendation to establish a national quality award. Instead, number 10 in the private sector initiatives recommendations suggested, "Establish a national medal for productivity achievement that would be awarded annually by the President of the United States for high levels of verifiable productivity achievement by organizations rather than individuals. Establish a commission to develop criteria and select the winners of such an award."[1]

In a report published by the American Productivity Center in 1983, a recommendation was included which spoke to the creation of a national quality award.[2] However, this recommendation stimulated no action on the part of the administration, and the recommendation was not included in the White House study's co-chairman's final report.

President Reagan keynoted the conference, and was followed by the then Vice President George Bush; then Secretary of Transportation Elizabeth Dole; the late Commerce Secretary Malcolm Baldrige, after whom the current award is named; Don Regan, then secretary of the treasury; and Ed Meese, then counselor to the president. Howard K. Smith, in his normal perceptive style, commented on the urgent need for us to get cracking and pointed out what the National Association of Broadcasters was doing in donating significant air time to accommodate the productivity "spots."

The report, entitled "Productivity Growth: A Better Life for America," was published in April of 1984 and contained some 82 recommendations for government action to improve productivity, and 66 private sector recommendations ranging from "managing information" to "technology."[3] I was puzzled about how this issue of establishing a national quality award, which I considered so important, had dropped out of the work the quality professionals had contributed.

Fortunately, the crusade did not end with that disappointment. In the fall of 1984, Dr. Jack Grayson was in Washington, D.C., and made an appointment to visit me in my Avco Corporation office. (Shortly after my retirement from the Navy, Avco invited me to become the corporate vice president, quality. I accepted, once assured that they were interested in establishing a quality culture in Avco's 11 major divisions, which ranged from basic research and aviation engines to high tech, electronics, insurance, and consumer finance.)

Recognizing that both of us had a common interest in the need to establish something that would motivate America toward greater heights of competitiveness, he suggested we join forces and work toward creation of, as Jack phrased it, "a national quality-productivity award." While I believed it should be single pronged, I was delighted to have a partner of Dr. Grayson's national stature and professional credentials.

Jack appointed one of his most dynamic staff members, Ms. Marty Russell, staff vice president for national affairs (and a definite rising star), to be his action officer. It was a professional marriage made in heaven I soon found out, as Marty possessed a very keen mind, plus indefatigable energy and determination bulldog–like in tenacity.

Actively supported by Jack, Marty quickly began to poll American Productivity Center supporters for their reaction to a presidential quality award, which included a straw man on what the criteria might include. In my Japanese Executive Study Tour (JEST) that fall, I posed the concept to Dr. Kaoru Ishikawa, president of Mushashi Institute of Technology and a member of Japan's Deming Prize committee. He reacted very positively, commenting only on why we were so late in getting such a concept implemented in America![4]

Marty and my Avco associate LCDR Ed Graham, USN (Ret), a Navy colleague and another steaming demon with a very keen mind, attended a conference in Cleveland of quality professionals in February 1985 to get their reaction to the award concept. They then worked throughout the spring and summer of 1985 getting input from the academic and industrial community.

By September 1985, Marty and Ed had sufficient support, which signaled a need to move ahead and "go public." The historic first formal meeting of the organizing group met in the conference room of Avco's Washington, D.C., office. Present at that meeting were Ed Graham from Avco; Jack Grayson and Marty Russell from APC; Dr. Bill Ruch of Arizona State University; Debra A. Owens, ASQC; Pat Townsend from Avco's Paul Revere Insurance Companies division; Bill Crosby and Dave Kennedy, American Airlines; Ray Smock, Ford Motor Co.; Tony Diamond, NASA; Charlie Mercer, McDonnell Douglas Electronics; Professor John Kendrick of George Washington University; and me. Ironically enough, this group consumed much of the first day's meeting discussing the name of the award. One segment insisted it should be the "quality-productivity award." But a number of us said that this would muddy up the waters, and the award should be focused on quality, which we pointed out produced the much-needed-by-America ingredient for increased productivity. The quality side of the discussion prevailed and the presidential quality award had its beginning—none of us ever fathoming that it would end up becoming a public law named after the then secretary of commerce and spare–time rodeo competitor, the honorable Malcolm "Mac" Baldrige.

One of the items discussed during the first two-day meeting was whether the award should be strictly for the private sector or open to the public sector. Additional discussion focused on whether the total corporation would have to apply or if divisions of a corporation could apply. Should it include both manufacturing and service companies, and, if both, would we need two separate criteria? Could individuals apply as they do in Japan? For starters, we settled on the private sector only; fiscal entities of corporations could apply; both manufacturing and service industries would be invited, and we would formulate a set of criteria that would satisfy both; and initially, there would be no provision for individuals to apply. At first, we examined 14 categories to be included in the criteria. The Deming Prize has 10 criteria, and we eventually ended up with seven.

Many of our original panel dropped out after that initial meeting, and the core group who met for the next two years consisted of Marty, who served as secretary; Ed; Pat; Debra; Ray; Tony; Charlie; D. L. "Bear" Baila,

Florida Power and Light; Joe Froelich, Campbell Soup; Dick Stimson and
Eli Lessor, Department of Defense; and Joe Cahalan, Xerox. I served as chair
of the group. Others contributed on a one- or two-time basis, but we were
the work horses who plodded forward, creating and refining the criteria,
establishing an organization, policy, administrative structure and procedures.
Jack Grayson, with his considerable influence in both the public and private
sector was the chief fund raiser and influencer of CEOs and high-ranking
government officials to become a part of this movement.

It looked like smooth sailing, until disaster struck. In late 1986, Debra
Owen was suddenly and without explanation withdrawn from participation
by ASQC headquarters. This followed John L. Hansel's (chairperson of the
board of ASQC) testimony to the House Subcommittee on Science,
Research, and Technology. He stated: "Is a national award what American
industry needs to be properly motivated to do something about quality
improvement? Are not the management and economic and national security motivations strong enough? Have these been properly articulated? Is the
concept of winning an award, which would give dubious marketing advantage to the winners, so compelling that a national award is necessary? If
there are winners, what about the losers? What happens if American Honda
wins the award? Is an award the best motivational strategy at our disposal?
We do not think so.

"At this stage of global competitiveness, I feel that the last thing
American industry needs is an internal competition for a national quality
award, especially since the award implies winners and losers. We need to
carefully and fully understand the proper context for a national award.

"The American Society for Quality Control would support and participate in an award process if it has the proper context. By that we mean a substantial technical assistance support program to provide guidelines, training,
and sharing of effective strategies with all industry and government."[5]

Ironically enough, our group understood the necessity for including the
elements Mr. Hansel spoke of, and had made provisions for them. We understood that the sharing of strategies, which allowed companies to successfully
compete against very difficult criteria, would be invaluable to companies
interested in improving their own competitiveness in the marketplace.

As for winners and losers, we believed that there would only be winners
since any firm competing for the award would be a winner if it introduced
the criteria elements into its quest for quality.

In October 1986, Dana Cound, the president of ASQC, responded to a
letter by Dr. Grayson asking why ASQC had withdrawn support. Cound

referred to John Hansel's statement before the House Committee in June, saying, "We have arrived at this position (of withdrawing support) after reviewing and analyzing our experience with the NASA Award, participation in Frank Collin's committee to develop your national award, and our testimony before Congress.

"While this policy precludes us from participating further in your award program at this time, I trust we can continue to explore areas of mutual cooperation."[6]

Withdrawal of ASQC participation and support caused many CEOs to question the desirability of continued association with the concept.

Meanwhile, even as "Bear" Baila of Florida Power and Light (FP&L) served on our committee to establish a national quality award (we had dropped the initial presidential quality award title), his boss, John J. Hudiburg, chairperson and CEO of FP&L, a dynamic quality zealot, encouraged Representative Fuqua of Florida to introduce House of Resolution 5321 (later known as HR 812), which would establish a national quality improvement award.

The House bill was supported by a Senate Resolution and on August 20, 1987, shortly after the tragic death of Malcolm Baldrige, President Reagan signed PL 100-107 creating the Malcolm Baldrige National Quality Award (MBNQA). The Department of Commerce under the Honorable C. William Verity, secretary of commerce, was assigned action. The National Bureau of Standards (now the National Institute of Science and Technology, NIST), directed by Ernest Ambler, was assigned responsibility for implementing PL 100-107. Within his staff, he charged Dr. Curt W. Reimann, then deputy director of the National Measurements Laboratory, to make it so. At this point, the survivors of our core group decided that we could do no less than offer the fruits of our labor to NBS to preclude them having to plow this same ground again. Dr. Reimann was happy to accept our offer and thus Marty Russell, Pat Townsend, Joe Froelich, "Bear" Baila, Charlie Mercer, Debra Owens, and I joined with the staff of NBS, which included, among others, George Uriano, Bert Coursey, Richard Franzen, Ruth Haines, and Helmut Hellwig to complete the project to which our original group had so assiduously applied our talents.

At our organization meeting at NBS in Gaithersburg on September 25, 1987, Dr. Ambler, dropped the other shoe.

"We have been directed to get this on the street as rapidly as possible, since the administration has declared that President Reagan will give the first awards in November 1988."

We all looked at each other in disbelief. After a hiatus of nine months as a result of ASQC's withdrawal of support, we were now expected to meet the original date our committee had established for the first presentation when we had created our original time sequence almost three years earlier.

Meanwhile, through the good offices of Douglas Eking, current president of ASQC, ASQC was back in the ball game. FP&L also came to the rescue and provided Alan Siebe from its staff full time to NBS. Marshall Herron, an ASQC director at large, was enlisted to help.

Since PL 100-107 stipulated that the MBNQA was to be funded from and managed by the private sector, on November 19, 1987, the ASQC board of directors voted to cooperate with the American Productivity Center to form a consortium that would handle this task. Each organization was to have three members on the board of directors. I was invited to be the seventh member. The chairmanship would rotate annually, and Doug Eking became the first chairman. The consortium contracted Robert Peach to serve as the operation's officer.

Through the astute management of the consortium and the work of Dr. Reimann of NIST, the application guidelines were on the street by February 15, 1988. The seven categories for the award examination were leadership, information and analysis, strategic quality planning, human resource utilization, quality assurance of products and services, results from quality assurance products and services, and customer satisfaction. These categories looked deeply into the applicant's organization, procedures, understanding, compliance, attitudes, operational and strategic planning for quality, and finally what the customer thought of the product or service he or she was receiving. Thorough? You bet!

Easy to achieve? Not on your life!

Anyone who successfully satisfied the initial three examiners' evaluation, followed by the senior examiners decision to make a site visit, and the judges' final approval of recommendation, ripped apart any cosmetic or paper quality program. Purposely made difficult in order that succeeding would be worthwhile and failing to achieve the standard would give the applicant an unbeatable chart by which to achieve competitive excellence through quality, the MBNQA has the potential for reestablishing America's standing as a quality-oriented producer of goods and services and a formidable competitor in world markets.

Sixty-six companies applied; 13 of these were finalists and three, Motorola, Commercial Nuclear Fuel Division of Westinghouse, and Globe

Metallurgical, were the jubilant winners of the first three Malcolm Baldrige National Quality Awards in 1988.

On November 14, 1988, at the White House, President Reagan presented the awards to Robert Galvin, chairman, Motorola Inc.; John C. Marous, chairman and CEO, Westinghouse Electric Corporation; and Arden C. Sims, president and CEO of Globe Metallurgical Inc., with the following words: "And today we salute three corporations that reflect American industry's dedication to quality. Each of them and thousands of others help keep America strong by making American products the best products available. They and others like them exemplify the belief that quality counts first, foremost, and always."

The dream had become reality!

## REFERENCES

1. William E. Simon, chairman, and L. William Seidman, co-chairman, White House Conference on Productivity, "Productivity Growth: A Better Life for America" (Washington, D.C., Department of Commerce, 1984), 76.

2. C. Jackson Grayson, "Computer Conferences on Productivity a Final Report for the White House Conference on Productivity" (Houston, Texas, American Productivity Center, 1983), 16–17.

3. William E. Simon, et al, *Op. Cit.*, 73, 86.

4. Twice each year—1984 through 1986, while vice president of quality, I guided Avco Corporation and Textron executives through a series of superbly managed Japanese industries to expose them to the successful management style of their chief competitors. In addition, we visited the then Ambassador Mansfield to get his views on Japan as the rising star of the Pacific basin area. We also visited Dr. Ishikawa, the Japan Productivity Center, and the Union of Japanese Scientists and Engineers (JUSE) to gain their insights into how Japan had overcome its economic problems following World War II. The tours, each two weeks in duration, never failed to drive home the deadly serious nature of our chief competitor.

5. Transcript of statement made by John L. Hansel to the House Subcommittee on Science, Research, and Technology on June 25, 1986.

6. Letter from Dana Cound, then president of ASQC, to C. Jackson Grayson dated October 3, 1986.

# BIBLIOGRAPHY

Abegglen, James C., and George J. Stalk, Jr. *Kaisha: The Japanese Corporation*. New York: Basic Books, 1985.

*ANSI/ASQC.ANSI/ASQC B1.1 (Guide for Quality Control Charts), B1.2 (Control Chart Method of Analyzing Data)*, and *B1.3 (Control Chart Method of Controlling Quality During Production)*. Milwaukee, Wis.: American Society for Quality Control, 1985.

Bradford, David L., and Allan R. Cohen. *Managing for Excellence*, New York: John Wiley & Sons, 1984.

Bureau of Business Practice. *ISO 9000: Handbook of Quality Standards and Compliance*. Waterford, Conn.: Bureau of Business Practice/Prentice Hall, 1992.

Camp, Robert C. *Benchmarking: The Search for Industry Best Practices That Lead to Superior Performance*. White Plains, N.Y.: Quality Resources and ASQC Quality Press, 1989.

Covey, Stephen R. *The Seven Habits of Highly Effective People*. New York: Fireside/Simon & Schuster, 1989.

Deming, W. Edwards. *The New Economics for Industry, Government, Education*. Cambridge, Mass.: MIT Press, 1993.

———. *Quality, Productivity, and Competitive Position*. New York: McGraw-Hill, 1982.

Drucker, Peter F. *Concept of the Corporation*. Boston: Beacon Press, 1960.

Dunn, Robert, and Richard Ullman. *Quality Assurance for Computer Software*. Cambridge, Mass.: Massachusetts Institute of Technology, 1982.

Feigenbaum, Armand V. *Total Quality Control*. 3d ed., rev. New York: McGraw-Hill, 1991.

Fliehman, Deborah G., and David D. Auld. *Customer Retention Through Quality Leadership: The Baxter Approach*. Milwaukee, Wis.: ASQC Quality Press, 1993.

Fukuda, Ryuji. *Managerial Engineering: Techniques for Improving Quality and Productivity in the Workplace*. Stamford, Conn.: Productivity Press, 1983.

Goldratt, Eliyahu M., and Jeff Cox. *The Goal*. 2d ed., rev. New York: North River Press, 1992.

Grayson, C. Jackson Jr., and Carla O'Dell. *American Business: A Two-Minute Warning*. New York: Free Press, 1988.

Ishikawa, Kaoru. *Guide to Quality Control*. Translated by the Asian Productivity Organization. Tokyo, Japan: Asian Productivity Organization, 1983.

————. *What Is Total Quality Control? The Japanese Way*. Translated by David J. Lu. Englewood Cliffs, N.J.: Prentice-Hall, 1985.

Juran, J. M., and Frank M. Gryna, Jr. *Quality Planning and Analysis*, 3d ed. New York: McGraw-Hill, 1993.

Miles, Lawrence D. *Techniques of Value Analysis and Engineering*. 2d ed. New York: McGraw-Hill, 1972.

Miller, Lawrence. *American Spirit*. New York: Warner Books, 1984.

QC Circle Headquarters, Union of Japanese Scientists and Engineers, ed. *How to Operate QC Circle Activities*, Tokyo, Japan: JUSE, 1985.

Schaeffer, Francis A., and C. Everett Koop. *Whatever Happened to the Human Race?* Old Tappan, N.J.: Flemming H. Revell Co., 1979.

Schmidt, Warren H., and Jerome P. Finnigan. *The Race Without a Finish Line.* San Francisco: Jossey-Bass Publishers, 1992.

Traver, Robert W. *Industrial Problem Solving: Isolating the Key Variables.* Carol Stream, Ill.: Hitchcock Publishing Co., 1989.

Trimble, Vance H. *Sam Walton: The Inside Story of America's Richest Man.* New York: Penguin Books, 1990.

Western Electric Co. *Statistical Quality Control Handbook.* 2d ed. Indianapolis, Ind.: AT&T, 1958.

Wilson, Paul F., Larry D. Dell, and Gaylord F. Anderson. *Root Cause Analysis: A Tool for Total Quality Management.* Milwaukee, Wisc.: ASQC Quality Press, 1993.

# INDEX